PICK UP THE CLAY

PICK UP THE CLAY
A Policeman's Life Journey

by

Shirley Elaine Stanelle

**Fame's Eternal Books, LLC
United States of America**

Copyright © 2021
Shirley Elaine Stanelle, author
Tammy L. Maté-Peterson and Larry D. Gensch, editors

ISBN: 978-1-7364346-2-8

All rights reserved. No part of this book may be reproduced or transmitted in any form by any means, electronic or mechanical, including photocopying, recording, or by any information storage and retrieval system, without written permission of the author or editors, except for the inclusion of brief quotations in reviews.

Printed in the UNITED STATES OF AMERICA

For additional information, contact:
Fame's Eternal Books, LLC at
TammyMate@aol.com

CONTENTS

PART ONE: First Journey
Chapter 1 I Killed a Man
Chapter 2 Waiting Room
Chapter 3 Recovery Room / The Mummy
Chapter 4 3:00 a.m.
Chapter 5 Thinking Back (Ken Becoming a Cop)
Chapter 6 Mickey Wakes Mommy / Ken's Folks
Chapter 7 Life-Changing Fight
Chapter 8 Thinking Back Again
Chapter 9 Reporters & Detectives
Chapter 10 Unwrapping The Mummy / Time for a Cigarette
Chapter 11 Ditties for the Nuns / Entertaining the Patients
Chapter 12 Lemons / Ken's Police Stories
Chapter 13 Our Dog, Freddie / Keystone Kops
Chapter 14 Getting Ready for Christmas
Chapter 15 Christmas at the Hospital
Chapter 16 An Unforgettable Rendezvous
Chapter 17 More Surgery / Cockroaches
Chapter 18 Cape Cod House / Stories for Cops
Chapter 19 Civic Heroism Award
Chapter 20 The Big Blow

PART TWO: Second Journey

Chapter 1 From Runaways to Prostitutes
Chapter 2 Beeper & Betty
Chapter 3 Working with Clay
Chapter 4 Selling Patterns at the Big New Jersey Show
Chapter 5 *Popular Ceramics* & CASH
Chapter 6 Ken's Inventions
Chapter 7 Deliveries by the Cerami-van
Chapter 8 A Step Forward—Renting a Shop
Chapter 9 Sebastiano Arrives
Chapter 10 Ever Popular / Traveling Teacher
Chapter 11 New Jersey Show / Blackout
Chapter 12 Wisconsin Horizons / Downward Dominoes / The Farm
Chapter 13 Corkies
Chapter 14 Business Expansion / Parties at the Farm
Chapter 15 Ken, the Entertainer
Chapter 16 Westward Bound – Colorado
Chapter 17 Native Americans / Colorado Wind Songs
Chapter 18 Santa's "Secret Gift Shop"
Chapter 19 A Surprise Visitor / Ever Involved / Blackouts
Chapter 20 Ken's Talk
Chapter 21 I Love You
Chapter 22 Ken's Legacy

I dedicate this book to the memory of my wonderful husband, Kenneth G. Stanelle. You taught me to believe in myself, Ken. You always made me feel good.

Ken was a professional policeman, potter, and lecturer; he was a mentor to many; but first and foremost, Ken loved his family and me.

I also dedicate this book to the many "blue" men and women police officers, who, *like my husband*, trained and learned to do their best at their job; and loved/love their job.

Shirley Elaine Stanelle

ACKNOWLEDGMENTS

My adult children kept hearing about the book, but it took so long. However, they still were available when I had to call on them for a technical answer. I am thankful to all of you: Michael, Peggy, David, and Penn. Penn, thank you for all the phone calling you made to check on exacting information. Thank you, Peggy, for working on the cover with me, and scanning and sending many items to Tammy. David and Michael, thank you for your expertise on mold-making—and Michael for being a part of the story.

I want to thank Larry Gensch for providing enlightening details and counseling on the fight. Larry was an impressionable teenager at the time, and he visited Ken at the hospital regularly. He heard the stories over and over again, and knows them well. I want to thank Elizabeth Moffett for her encouragement—telling me to "keep going" after she read the first copy of the manuscript. *Thank you, Elizabeth.* My friend, Jean Del Monico came to our cabin for a week; and while she was there, she read my manuscript on the computer. She was full of encouragement, and told all her friends that they definitely will want to read my book. *Thank you, Jean.* I want to thank my grandson, Julian Stanelle, for reading and editing, and adding his comments on the side of the paper. *Thank you, Julian.* I want to thank Rick Lunn for taking the time to listen to four of the tapes, and picking out the best one of "Ken's Talk" to include in the book. *Thank you, Rick.*

Thanks to all the people that came to the reading of *Ken's Talk*. Many of those present had actually heard Ken when he gave his talk while creating a pot on his wheel.

Last, but not least, many thanks to Tammy Maté-Peterson, my editor and publisher, for understanding the man even though she never met him, and for guiding me along the way.

Shirley Elaine Stanelle
Author

EDITOR'S NOTE

When Shirley approached my father, Larry D. Gensch, and asked him if I could publish Ken's story, I accepted wholeheartedly, and began with great zeal. I had grown up listening to my grandparents (Ed and Roberta Gensch) speak with the highest regard of both Ken and Shirley. I knew that they loved and respected them immensely, and that my dad felt the same.

During the year that I edited and published *Pick Up The Clay*'s 2017 edition, Shirley e-mailed me almost weekly—urging me to speed up the process. She approached the age of 90, and feared she would never see it in print. I skipped several steps, and published it faster than any book ever before. In doing so, although Ken's story is *amazing* no matter how it is told, I felt disappointed with the quality I like to provide. I am a perfectionist.

In this 2021 version of *Pick Up The Clay*, I have adapted Ken's life story for both visual learners and aural learners. As a teacher of many years, I know how important this is. For those who will read this aloud to aural learners, I have embedded visual cues. You will find some in brackets, or as italicized words. Actors and community theater performers, such as myself, also appreciate this.

First, I want to express my deepest gratitude to Shirley Stanelle, *and my guardian angels* (Ed, Roberta, and Ken?), for this fantastic experience. Second, I want to thank my dad, Larry Douglas Gensch, for helping me edit the most important part of the book—the fight story. He, like Shirley, had heard the fight story firsthand many, many times; but as a military man himself, he understood the logistics much more profoundly than either Shirley or I. Third, I want to thank my mom, Barbara Sue Gensch, for providing excellent commentary. Finally, I want to thank my husband, John Thomas Peterson, for providing his expertise at proofreading.

Tammy Lyn Maté-Peterson
Editor and Publisher

PREFACE

My story is about my husband, Kenneth Stanelle, honorable policeman for the Milwaukee Police Department. One Thanksgiving night, an event occurred that changed our lives forever. Many times things happen, and we have to start over again. Sometimes it is harder the second or third time around. Ken fervently wanted to serve people of all types. He had to find new ways.

Ken was asked, *repeatedly*, to write his story; and he always assured everyone he would get to it. But, he passed away before he finally got started on it. I can't write "his" story, but I am the narrator in the story, and this is his story told through me.

Shirley Elaine Stanelle
Author

FOREWORD

"How you grade me is unimportant. When you are down there, and feel you are in the gutter, and don't think you have a friend; just remember these four words:

                PICK UP THE CLAY."

                                    Kenneth Stanelle

PART ONE:

First Journey

As told by Kenneth Stanelle's wife, Shirley Elaine Stanelle

CHAPTER ONE

It was 10:45 on Thanksgiving night 1957, and I was ironing and watching television in the living room. The children were in bed, the Thanksgiving dishes were finished and put away, and I was happy for the chance to watch the movie "Singing in the Rain" (with Gene Kelly) while catching up with the laundry. The screen of the TV was 15 inches, *but it worked*—and anyway, it was all we could afford.

My husband, Ken, was a Milwaukee policeman working the three to eleven shift, and I always waited up for him, and watched TV, read, or folded clothes, fresh from the dryer. Or like tonight, I decided to iron. I smiled as I moved the steam iron along his shirt. Since he was advanced to a plain-clothes officer, the white shirt was a lot easier to finish than the god-awful, stiff, blue uniform that had to be starched and ironed with two vertical creases down the back and front. *"Just like the Army,"* I thought. He had a friend, Harold, on the force that was divorced, and took his shirts to a laundry. *"How could he afford that?"*

I pictured Ken with the new felt hat I had given him for an anniversary present. I hoped it would keep his head warm, because the outside temperature was cold. The wind chill factor was two below, and it would get colder before the night was over. I could not help getting excited when I coyly thought to myself, *"Well, now I'll just have to warm him up when he gets home."*

I loved going to bed with him, and feeling his body cuddling around mine. The heat and love from his body could instantly chase away any chills—with pajamas on or off!

Ken said he and Bill might stop by during a break to get another helping of the strawberry shortcake I had made. It was going to be a slow night, because all the taverns were supposed to be closed on Thanksgiving.

His partner, Bill, doesn't always like to stop; but I know Ken likes his breaks, so he can have his cigarette.

"Where the heck were they anyway? They must have stopped somewhere else."

I was almost finished with ironing when the doorbell rang. Freddy, our Labrador, stood, woofed, and looked at me.

"Well, they must be here, but why didn't they just come in? Ken must have forgotten his key."

It did happen once before, and maybe the big dinner and strawberry shortcake clouded his thinking, and he forgot to grab it on his way out.

"But wait a minute. He would have come in the back door if he was coming home."

Our apartment was near downtown Milwaukee, and we had numerous latches on the front door. I was used to living in the country or a small town, where doors were always open and unlatched. Freddy followed me to the door, waiting to see who it was. I put on the porch light, finally got the door opened, and was surprised to see Sergeant Every standing there.

There had been times before when Ken had landed in the hospital because of a fight or a scuffle, and this was not the first time an officer had visited my doorstep in the late hours. But I was startled as I peered up at him, because he was shifting uneasily, and his eyes looked so sad—even though he stood at attention, straight and tall.

I held the door open for him, and he entered. Freddy relaxed, because he was used to seeing a uniform, and the sergeant put his hand on Freddy's head.

"Mrs. Stanelle...."

Just the way he spoke and looked, I knew this was different.

"Is he alive?" I asked.

"Yes," he quietly replied, "I'll take you to the hospital."

For a moment, I became nauseous; but it seemed when something serious happened, my inner strength always kicked in.

"I'll have to run next door, and have my neighbor come over to watch the children," I told him.

This was not the first time I was escorted to the hospital. I didn't let myself think what could have happened. It had never been too serious before. I grabbed my jacket from the hall tree, and hurried out. I rang Susie's doorbell, standing there jiggling up and down, and saying to myself, *"Hurry...hurry...."*

She soon came to the door in her nightgown.

"Susie," I nervously said, "I need you to watch Mickey and the baby while I go to the hospital. I'm sorry to bother you so late."

Trying to fathom what I was talking about in her half sleep, she said, "Sure, Hon, what's wrong?"

"I don't know, but you know Ken.... Got himself hurt again at work," I answered.

She put on her bathrobe and slippers, threw her jacket over her shoulders, and followed me.

"And Susie?" I was asking her as we hurried, "If the baby wakes up, I think there's a bottle already made up.... *I hope."*

"You just don't worry about those little ones. I'll take care of them."

Susie was one of those people you could visualize as a favorite aunt—a little on the chunky side, round face with pink cheeks, a big smile, and *always* with a hearty laugh.

The Sergeant was still standing inside the door where I left him. Luckily, I was wearing warm corduroy pants and a heavy sweater; so all I had to do was zip up my jacket, and follow him to the squad car.

Not a word was spoken on the way to the hospital. I couldn't find words, and I knew from experience that *he* couldn't elaborate either. Even though I was warm enough in the squad car, I was so nervous I was shivering as though I was frozen. The hospital seemed grim, as well—especially when it holds so many sad or unhappy stories. We proceeded to the elevator, and I felt even smaller standing next to this tall, uniformed man. My courage was diminishing. And still not a word was spoken between us. Just silence.

The quiet was soon to end, because when we got to the third floor, there was so much activity with policemen in the hall, and nurses and doctors running back and forth. And then I was ushered into this tiny room. Maybe it was not tiny, but there were so many people in there.

What I saw at a glance was a bloody person lying in the bed, our minister sitting on the other side of him, and the room full of people—doctors, nurses and a police recorder.

I stepped into the room, and Ken lay there with bandages on his face. When he saw me, his eyes filled with tears—not from pain, but anguish and sorrow.

Before I could even say anything, he whispered, "Hon, I killed a man."

This was different from any other time. This was serious. Especially when he added, "They just finished taking my '*dying*' statement."

Through my tears I thought, *"They called our minister before me?"* Then I heard someone say they had wanted to reach me before the late news came on.

It seemed like everyone was speaking at once…. "He has just given his dying statement…." "We have to get him to the operating room…." "No…we don't know about Bill." "You will have to wait in the waiting room…."

My head was buzzing. Reverend Cramer came to my side, and put his arm around me; and I'm glad he did, or I may have passed out.

The Reverend was saying a prayer. "Lord, we ask that you watch over Kenneth…."

Then they wheeled him away.

Reverend Solomon G. Cramer
(February 10, 1914 - January 1, 2013)
His adult life centered on ministry in the
United Methodist Church, and he was the longest
serving clergy in the Wisconsin Conference.

CHAPTER TWO

A nurse's aide hustled me out of Ken's room, and led me to the waiting room, because the specialist who was going to try to put Ken's handsome face back together had just arrived. I didn't know how bad it was. Reverend Cramer joined me, and we prayed and waited. I wasn't given any details—just that Ken and his partner, Bill, had been in a knife and gun fight.

I got up, and used the phone in the waiting room, and called our friends. We were close with Roberta and Ed Gensch. We met them when we first moved to Milwaukee, and settled into one of the apartments that Cousin Al could let us occupy….
[*I drifted into thought….*]

> Shortly after we moved in, there was a knock on the door. Ken had answered, and a couple stood there smiling and saying, "Welcome to Milwaukee!"
> To say the least, we were shocked, but invited them in, and offered our couch to sit down on.
> They were from our church. The first thing we did when we arrived in Milwaukee was find a church. We found a Methodist church we were comfortable with, and signed our names as guests. Roberta and Ed were the *Welcomers*. Our friendship grew, and we became lasting friends….

[*Back to reality….*]
I called Ed, and didn't tell him much, but he just said, "I'll be right there."

I was glad I knew their number, and could call them. I sat down again by Reverend Cramer. "Oh, my God," I exclaimed while poking Reverend on his arm to get his attention. "I'll have to call his folks."

They lived about 100 miles north of the City in Seymour, and I could anticipate my mother-in-law's anger toward me. When Ken first told her he was going to be a police officer, she hollered at me. "Why did you let him do that? Don't you know he could get killed?"

What she didn't know or understand was that I was so hung up on this guy that whatever he did that could make him happy was okay by me.

I couldn't help think back about our life together. We were so young, and yet had done so much....
[*I drifted into thought again.*]

> I remember when Ken left for the Army in 1945, and I cried myself to sleep. I was a senior in a small town high school. He had been a cook and baker in the service, and continued his schooling in baking when he returned home. We were married, and shortly after found ourselves owning a bakery. Talk about being pretty smug! Twenty-one years old and in business! The celebration of our Grand Opening ended up with me crawling up the stairs to bed giggling, with Ken following after me, poking and grabbing. Our lovemaking was always a *masterpiece,* and that night it produced an addition to our family.

Suddenly the door opened, and Reverend and I jumped up. But it was the nurse's aide bringing us some coffee.

"Thanks," I answered, looking up appreciatively.

The coffee tasted wonderful; and because I really couldn't engage in small talk, I slipped back into my thoughts....

> The bakery business was short-lived; and we found ourselves moving to Milwaukee, where a cousin offered to get Ken a job at A.O. Smith Manufacturing, where he worked — and had a hefty two-week check to prove it. Another cousin

had a number of three-story houses, which he made into apartments for rent. He rented one unit to us for only $80.00 a month if we would take care of the place. We basically had to rent the apartments out, collect the money, and clean them whenever a tenant moved out.

But I got to thinking about the single room in the front of our apartment. It was rented to "Jake" who had been there four years, and Cousin Al didn't want to turn him out. But I had to clean it, and it really made me mad when he peed in the wastebasket.

He was drunk half the time, but what really took the cake was the location of his room to our bedroom. Imagine his room as the original parlor, and our bedroom as the dining room with a sliding door between. Only this "door" was permanently closed. Well anyway, when Ken and I were enjoying each other in bed, and could hear a cough from the next room, I would freeze.

"Ken, he's listening! I can't go on." I could imagine him jacking off to the sound of our bed jumping.

I hated that man.

CHAPTER THREE

Moments later, the door opened again, and Ed came in. Reverend Cramer got up, and he and Ed shook hands.

"Hi Reverend," Ed greeted him.

"Ed, good you could come down," Reverend responded. "As soon as Kenneth is out of surgery, and we know how things are, perhaps you could stay with Shirley, and then take her home."

"You bet," Ed said.

Our conversation was interrupted when I realized someone had come into the room. I jumped, and ran to Bill's wife. We embraced.

"Oh, Helen, isn't it awful? How is Bill?"

Bill was Ken's partner ever since they went plain-clothes.

We sat down, and she quietly said, "I don't know. A nurse went by me in the hall, and I overheard her tell another one that he didn't make it…. But no one has told me anything."

We all held hands, and said a prayer for Bill with Reverend Cramer.

Bill was tall, handsome, and quiet. Sometimes, it seemed he was withdrawn. He gave the appearance of authority. He was a good partner for Ken.

Helen was an old-time, good person—pretty in a motherly way. She not only raised her own children, but her sister's daughter as well. She was polite and quiet, and devoted to her family. She had a day job in an office, and Bill's mother took care of the children while she was at work. Helen certainly was not one who would run after the nurses, and demand to know what was going on.

****

It seemed forever before a nurse came in, and said, "Mrs. Stanelle, you can see your husband now in the recovery room."

I gave Helen a hug, and I started to follow the nurse. But then I said, "Wait, can't you find out something about Helen's husband?"

She stopped, and turned; and with eyes full of pity, softly responded, "I'll try...."

Reverend and Ed joined me as we hurried down the hall. We turned left, then right again, and finally got to the elevators. We pushed the second floor button, more hallways, and by now I am so nervous, my heart is starting to pound. We finally stopped, and followed the nurse into a room.

The nurse pulled back the curtain. There he lay. My hero. His head was completely wrapped like a mummy with openings for his eyes, nostrils, and a slit for his mouth—just room enough for a straw to be used to sip up JELL-O. Ken's jaw had been wired, and it would be a lot of days before he could eat solid food again.

When he saw me, tears welled up in his eyes—as well as in mine. But he was breathing....

He was alive.

I kissed his hands, and then held them tight. He was trying to whisper something, and we finally understood his whispering. "Is Bill alright?"

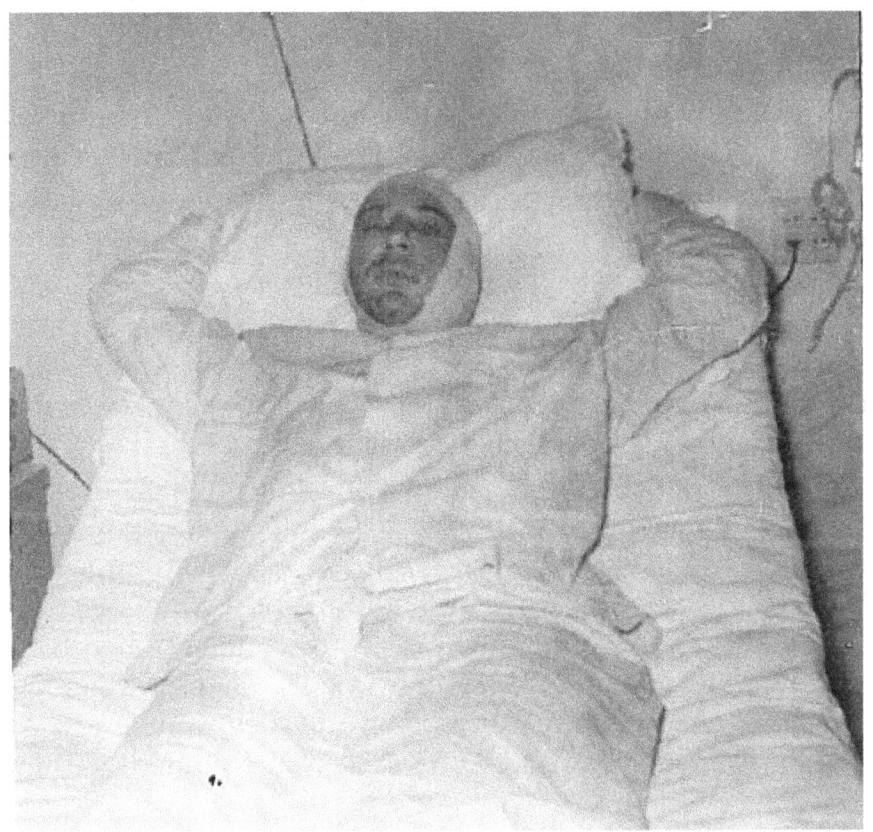
Ken, a few days after our visit

Reverend Cramer had to leave, but first spoke with Ken a few minutes, and assured both of us that our church was there to help in any way they could…and then he left.

A doctor came in, and between him and a police officer who was standing by, gave bits and pieces of the tragic story. The doctor told me Ken's ear had been cut off, and put back on; his jaw broken; his saliva gland had been severed during the ten-inch slash of the left side of Ken's face and throat. Two hundred eighty-one stitches put him back together.

The policeman then told the short version of what happened, but Ken helped put together the fully-detailed story the following day.

The policeman provided the police department's perspective. He told how the station got a call on the callbox, shouting the address; and help was sent immediately....

> The first squad car there witnessed a man on his knees. He described him as "dressed in a topcoat, bloody beyond recognition, waving a gun to the crowd of people on the sidewalk, and shouting his police number."
> They then realized it was a detective, and the partner was on the ground pumping out blood from his arterial vein. Two other men were laying on the ground. One man appeared dead, and the other moaning and holding his leg.
> The police had a hard time being professional when they saw what they assumed had happened. There was blood running to the gutter along the street, and they were angry.
> They immediately had *"The Hole"* surrounded. They questioned everyone.
> Meanwhile, ambulances rushed Bill and Ken to the nearest hospital. Ken's left hand was still holding his throat together, and his gun was riveted to his right hand. No one could remove *either* until the Sergeant arrived to the hospital room, and shouted, "Officer Stanelle, hand over that gun! It's over!"

A nurse came in, just as the policeman in Ken's hospital room finished the short version of the story. She whispered to the doctor, and the doctor shared the good news. Bill had survived.

We later learned that Bill had been knifed from the knee to the groin, cutting a main artery which downed him immediately. He lost so much blood; there hadn't been much hope for him. But when the ambulance got him to the hospital, someone remembered that a famous surgeon from out of town had just finished giving a lecture on repairing arteries at a different hospital that evening. That hospital was on the other side of the city; but the surgeon was called, and Officer Anthony Scarvonsio took off to get him.

The doctor, waiting at the front door, hopped into the squad car, and got the ride of his life. With red lights flashing and sirens blaring, the racecar- wannabe skidded into park by Misericordia Hospital with a blown radiator. The doctor jumped out, was taken to surgery, and he repaired the artery.

He saved Bill's life.

CHAPTER FOUR

It was 3 o'clock in the morning, and I knew I had to get home, and be ready for Ken's folks. They would be at our place in just a few hours. I squeezed Ken's hands, but the medication had already put him to sleep. The doctor assured me he would be heavily medicated until the next day, so I told Ed I was ready for a ride home; but I wanted to check on Helen first, and he was patient, and waited.

I found Helen still in the previous waiting room, and I ran over to her saying, "Did you hear? Bill made it."

They had just told her, and she was waiting to go to the recovery room to see him. Her family had joined her, so she wasn't alone. I told her goodnight, and left.

Ed drove me home, walked me to the door, and waited for me to get inside. When I got inside, Susie offered to stay the rest of the night, but I assured her I would be okay. She said she would be back in the morning, so I could go to the hospital again. We both peeked in at the baby, and she was still sleeping.

Susie was a good soul and a good neighbor. She always looked jolly. A little overweight, she got a kick out of finding some mod outfit that would make her look cool. She had natural curly hair, and she and her husband had a good marriage. Sometimes she would come over, and we would have a cup of coffee and a snack, and we would yak about our husbands. She would pick up the baby, and sing to her; and Mickey thought she was the *cat's pajamas.*

After Susie left, I sat down at the kitchen table, put my head down, and wailed. The tears came pouring out, and I could not stop. I had held it in until my stomach ached, and my head felt like it would burst.

I just couldn't hold it in any longer.

CHAPTER FIVE

I was exhausted after that, and went to bed. Too wound up, I could not sleep; so I got up again.

I needed to learn the full details of the fight story. I needed to know exactly what had happened to my handsome, wonderful husband!

It was going to be a busy day in the morning when Ken's folks arrived. Perhaps a glass of milk would help. I poured a glass of milk, and sat looking at the paper I had left on the table. That brought back memories of the day seven years ago when Ken and I were reading the morning paper together.... [*I drifted back in time....*]

"Honey, listen to this!" Ken excitedly said, "The police department is accepting applications for police patrolmen; and applications can be picked up at the Safety Building on Ninth and State any day of the week. Testing will begin next month."

He looked at me, and said, "I've got to try it; and if I don't try now, I won't be able to live with myself."

Ken hated the job his cousin got for him working at A.O. Smith Corp. He complained it was too easy, and not enough to do. His job was to inspect airplane propellers, *or rather,* inspect their location in the plant to see how far they moved during the shift.

He devised a new schedule sheet; and after a few weeks, he knew where every propeller was located just by looking at the clock. When he talked to the foreman, he told him about his new schedule sheet, and asked for something more to do. The foreman pointed to a box at the end of the building, and said, "That might keep you busy!"

When Ken went there, and lifted the cover, he found a box full of magazines and comic books.

Ken often told how his dad taught him that whenever you think you know it all, that's when you'll find out just how stupid you are. So much for self-initiative.... But it was a paycheck, and we were both appreciative of that.

When we had the bakery, Ken started at 3:00 a.m.; *midnights* on Fridays. It was during those night hours that his interest in police work was established. The local police officers and the state police would stop by for donuts and coffee — *and* to shoot the breeze. Sometimes he would lock up, and tag along in the state patrol car for a short drive. There wasn't much activity in a small town, but they could always hope for something, or *anything,* to happen. All of these officers seemed like normal people to Ken, and not police.

Another time that was really a *deciding* time for him was on a Saturday morning. On Saturdays, when the late shift got off work in Milwaukee, he would go with his cousin Rube, and stop at Johnny's Round Up to have a bucket of beer, cash their checks, and play Sheepshead — a Milwaukee card game.

That Saturday morning, he came home a little earlier than usual. He was so excited; he couldn't wait to tell me what happened at Johnny's.

Now understand, we both were a little green behind the ears as far as living in a big city was concerned; and we would be surprised about *people in general* many times in the future.

Ken started telling me about a character who hung out at Johnny's. He was in his mid-fifties, with just a few teeth that belonged to him; and he wore an old, brown overcoat the year round. Everyone just called him Smitty, and someone would always buy him a beer...

Smitty would walk up to your table, and come out with some little gimmick item, like a deck of cards with nude women on them, or a key chain with a big screw attached that had a disc with the word YOU on it. *That was pretty easy to figure out.* He would sell these items to the guys in the bar.

That morning, they were playing cards, and Ken said he couldn't have won with a marked deck. Smitty was making his rounds of the tables, and Ken went to the bar for a sausage sandwich. While Ken was washing it down with a beer, he noticed Smitty walk over to a table where two guys were playing Tonk Poker. The two men were new, it seemed, but had on grease-stained coveralls, and were in their mid-thirties.

Ken could not hear them amid the din in the bar; but as usual, Smitty was hustling them into buying something he had. After only a few words, the two men quietly got up from the table, and Smitty walked outside with them.

Ken left to start home, and in walking past the alley, witnessed Smitty against the wall of the building; and the two men were searching him. They turned him around, and guided him into the back seat of a blue Ford sedan. Ken noticed that they had handcuffs on him. One man got in with him, and the other drove. Turning quickly into the morning traffic, they were soon lost to view.

"My God," Ken said, "It was a *pinch*, and the two guys must have been *detectives*."

Shivers ran up Ken's back, both in fear and excitement. He caught the streetcar; and all the way home, it was going through his mind how deadly smooth and effective the whole thing went—not the kind of *Shoot'em up, Bang! Bang!* that detective magazines and T.V portrayed.

Ken was so lost in thought, he almost missed his stop. He jumped off the streetcar, hurried to our apartment, and could hardly wait to tell me all about it.

It was after telling me this story, that Ken gravely said, "I want to be a cop."

****

Ken worked the night shift; so Monday morning, right after breakfast, he left to take the bus downtown to the Safety

Building to pick up his application. It was April, and for the first time in many years, spring was early; and though the nights were cool, it stayed warm and humid during the day. He returned about two hours later, a little deflated. He had walked in, and asked the policeman behind the counter for an application.

"Go across the hall, and fill it out!"

Across the hall, Ken noticed four other men bending over their papers; but when he started on his own application, he was a little disappointed. It wasn't any different than *most* applications; and when he took it back to the desk, the officer just stated "Put it in the basket."

Ken unceremoniously threw it in a basket on the counter, and walked away. Now that he finished that, he was sure it was over.

I felt bad for him, because I hated seeing him so disappointed. It is wonderful to have a dream to think about, and not so wonderful to have it taken away.

Then one morning, there was a letter in the mail from the Police Department, and I gave it to Ken to open. We were both excited, but it was just a form letter saying that on Saturday, April 16th, there would be a written test for the position of Patrolman in Room 300 at the Safety Building. Ken said he wasn't excited about it, but I could see the adrenaline building up. He confessed that he would go through with it, even though he felt it so remote to think a small-town boy invading a metropolitan police force of over a thousand men could *qualify*. In fact, he felt downright foolish.

I had my work cut out for me. I had to keep his enthusiasm up.

****

Saturday morning came, and I was not able to send him off with good wishes for his written test. He worked until 7:00

a.m., and had to be downtown by 8:00 a.m.; so he went right from work.

When he came home later, and told me about it; I had to keep from *laughing* to myself.

He got lost in the building, and finally stopped a policeman in the almost vacant corridor, and asked him where Room 300 was.

The policeman looked at him, and said, "On the *third* floor, Mac."

Poor Ken was so embarrassed at his own stupidity—as he called it. He finally found the assembly room full of men, and the Police Sergeant handed him his written examination....

"Shirl, this sergeant merely told me to leave it blank if I didn't know the answer! Then he went into big detail to tell me about the questions.... 'If the questions are *True or False*, then use the letters T & F. On the multiple choice, circle the letter of the correct answer.' Just typical high school stuff!" Ken complained.

Then Ken moaned, "I'm not going to pass! The first ten questions all pertained to City Government: 'Who is the Mayor of Milwaukee?' *I sure didn't know or care, so I skipped that one.* Then, 'Who is the District Attorney? Who is your Alderman? What ward did I live in?'"

Then Ken added, "And these *shoes*.... Where did we buy them? They made a *clopping* noise when I walked up front with my test, and some S.O.B. gave me a *wolf* whistle."

Poor guy, not only did Ken feel all alone; but he had worked all night, so he was really tired. I had made a mistake, too....
I heard him coming up the front steps, went out to greet him, and asked, "Well, how did it go?"

"A bunch of bullshit!" he angrily replied. He stormed in, and went to bed.

Of course, I hadn't helped the situation by answering with ice dripping in my words, *"Sorry I asked."*

Later, when he got up, we both apologized for our statements. Then I went shopping, and bought an evening paper. It had a picture of the men taking the test. It read, "347 Take Police Exam." I handed the paper to Ken, and he glumly said, "With that many guys, what chance do I have?"

I was *wise* for a change, and didn't answer him. Instead, I scooted Mickey toward him, and their playtime took *all* the pressure off.

The next two weeks dragged by. Finally, a letter came from the police department. I wanted to open it, but it would be *special* for Ken to open it.

When he came home, I handed him the letter, and Ken asked, "Why didn't *you* open it, so you could *prepare* me?"

"Well, honey, it was addressed to you, and I was nervous too; and anyway, I wanted *you* to get to open it."

Ken tore open the envelope, and silently read the letter. [*Here is what the letter said:*]

Dear Mr. Stanelle,

We congratulate you on passing the written examination for Police Patrolman. Your score of 83 places you 26th on the exam. We request that on May 18th you appear at the Safety Building gymnasium to take the physical examination. Should you have any questions regarding this examination, please call 461-2525 and ask for SGT Layman.

Sincerely,

Captain King

"Tell me...tell me!" I yelled.

He hollered, "I made it!" and as he picked me up, and twirled me around, he added, "I'm in!"

He was happy—I was happy.

****

My head slid forward, and bumped the table. I then realized I had fallen asleep while sitting up; so I got up, and crawled to bed. It was 5:00 a.m., and I knew Ken's folks would start out at about 6:00, and could be here by 8:30. I would make coffee first thing when I got up, and I had eggs and bread on hand for a change, so could make toast and scrambled eggs....

With those thoughts, I finally drifted off to sleep.

CHAPTER SIX

"Mommy, Mommy, *MomMom!!!* Wake up!" Mickey shook my shoulders trying to get me awake.
"The door bell is ringing, and someone is knocking on the door. And.... *Where is Daddy?*"

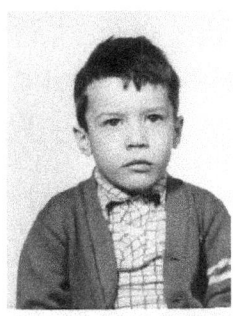

27TH STREET
SCHOOL DAYS 55-56
Mickey Stanelle

I struggled to come to, and realized that it was my son shaking me...and then I heard the knocking on the front door. I was still dressed from the night before; so I jumped up, and started running. My in-laws were standing there getting cold, and probably worried that I would never get there before they *froze* to death. I swung the door open; and Mickey was jumping up and down shouting, "Grandma, Grandpa.... Yeah!"

I apologized, invited them in, and led them to the kitchen. They took off their coats, and hung them on the backs of the chairs. While I was explaining about my oversleeping, I got the coffee out, and filled the coffee maker with water. My head still wasn't working right, and Mickey kept saying, "Where is *Daddy?*"

He was concerned, because normally when he woke up, Ken would let him jump on him in bed, or help him get dressed, and have breakfast with him before he went to Kindergarten.

"You know what? Run and get your clothes, and I'll help you get dressed; and then I'll tell you."

He ran off, and soon returned with his clothes— his black corduroy pants and a red sweatshirt with a funny truck printed on it—one of his favorites. *Grandma Delma* helped him get his pajamas off and clothes on, while *Grandpa Grover* winked at him, made faces, and smoked his pipe. Ken's mom and dad were in their late 60's, putting on a little extra weight, and looking and acting the part of loving grandparents—which they were. They both just loved babies and little children.

Mickey's excitement woke up Peggy, and she must have been wondering why she was being ignored. I picked her up; and Mom asked me to bring diapers, so she could change her. I handed the baby to Mom, and lifted Mickey up to the table. He grabbed his new shoes with the new shoe ties. He had been learning to tie his shoes, and so I made a big production about his new skills.

"I have something I have to tell you, honey. Daddy was in a very serious accident, and is hurt, and in the hospital. That's why Grandma and Grandpa are here, so I can take them to the hospital to see him."

"Can I go too?" he asked.

"I think you can, and we'll hope the hospital will let you in to see him. He's all bandaged up, just like a mummy. I'll leave Peggy with Susie."

The coffee was finished, and toast had popped up; so I quickly scrambled some eggs, and we sat down. I told Mom and Dad Stanelle what I knew, which wasn't a complete picture; and of course, they were more sad and concerned than angry at me.

I put a bottle on to get warm for Peggy, and excused myself for a moment, to go to the porch to see if the paper had come, which it had.

We all stared as I laid it on the table.

The headline across the top of the Milwaukee Journal was glaring:

CHAPTER SEVEN

We finished breakfast, and Susie came over to take baby Peggy to her apartment. Dad and Mom Stanelle were anxious to see Ken—and as anxious as I was to learn the details of the fight. We bundled up, and climbed in our old Hudson, and I drove to the hospital. We lived near the center of Milwaukee, and the hospital was closer to the *west* side.

We got to the hospital, and found out Ken's room number. He and Bill had been moved to the same room—number 311. We took the elevator to the third floor, and headed down the hall.

It was not hard to miss. Police officers were going in and out of the room, including the Chief. One officer sat outside the room as a guard. The room was full of flowers. The Sisters found space on windowsills, dressers, and even brought in an extra table to hold more plants. They were from individuals and floral shop businesses that were in their precincts.

The uniform officers mostly brought cigarettes. Ken still chain-smoked, but Bill quit one night when they were in the squad car, and stopped to get a cup of coffee....

> Bill went to the cigarette vending machine, and stopped dead in front of it. "Twenty-five cents a pack!" he yelled. "It was nineteen cents last week.... *I QUIT!*"

And he did. Never had another cigarette from that day on.

****

We entered Room 311, and immediately went to Ken's side near the window, and gave him a hug. I made room for his folks to get close to express their concerns. I picked up Mickey, put him on the bed, and he just stared and stared. It must have been pretty scary to see a *mummy* in place of someone he loved.

That was until Ken reached out, and held his hand. Those big, huge, tender hands helped Mickey know it was his daddy, *indeed*. Meanwhile, I went to the other bed; and gave Bill a hug, and Helen one, too.

The door opened, and one of the nuns came in carrying a big basket. It was full of get-well cards and good wishes. That continued every day with more and more cards. The city had been traumatized by all this, and they were standing by their police officers!

Then Captain Sprague came in, and a nun took Mickey out to entertain him. With Mickey gone, all had questions. What Ken and Bill pieced together from each other's perspective, and from witnesses, was this story. The story I had been waiting for.

It was break time, and Ken said, "Let's head over to my apartment for strawberry shortcake! We still have some left over from Thanksgiving dinner."

Bill said, "Okay, but let's drive through *The Hole* on our way, and make sure no one is open. You know that Old Mill Tavern down there likes to do things *their* way."

The Hole was an area that was located next to the train tracks on Canal Street, and in a crummy area of the city.

"Crap!" Ken complained, "There goes our strawberry shortcake!"

Bill laughed, and commented, "Stanelle, you're *always* hungry."

In the dim light, as Ken and Bill approached the Old Mill Tavern (at 2908 W. Greves Street), they observed people coming out of the door. They could make out two men beginning to drag a third man between them; a woman in a green coat followed close behind.

Ken and Bill pulled over, got out of the unmarked car, and approached the group showing their badges.

"What's going on here?" asked Ken.

"Nuts to you, copper. You ain't goin' to take me in!" one man answered.

"We aren't making an arrest," Ken said. "We simply want to know what's going on."

Suddenly, the man in the middle, *Washington*, hauled off and hit Ken.

"It's a set up!" Ken thought.

Bill moved in behind Washington, and grabbed him in a Half Nelson while reaching back for his handcuffs. Just then, the thug named Thompson swung at Ken, and struck him in the face.

The sounds at the time were a large thump of one man dropping, the grunts from those in the fight, and the screams and shouts from the women bystanders on the curb.

Ken pushed Thompson back, and heard Bill yell, "Ken, help!"

Ken turned, and saw Bill on the ground with Washington holding a large knife over him. Bill was bleeding profusely from a leg wound—from knee to groin through a main artery.

"For God's sake, stop him!" Bill yelled.

Ken pulled his service revolver, and shot the assailant Washington in the knee.

Thompson rushed at Ken, and they slugged it out—so hard that it knocked one of Thompson's shoes off.

The woman picked up the size-13 shoe with steel cleat on the heel, and started pounding Ken on the head with it.

Ken pushed the bitch back.

He then saw a flash in front of his face, as he was being hit again. His face stung as though a hot poker had touched him. It was Thompson.

Ken pushed Thompson back, and then felt air coming into his mouth through his cheek.

"He's been slashing me with a knife!" Ken realized.

Thompson's next charge was met with the butt of Ken's gun on the top of his head.

The knife *still* found its target.

Ken reached his hand up to the side of his head, and realized that most of his ear dangled, only slightly attached. He felt queasy and disoriented as Thompson spun around, and charged again, with knife in hand. This time, Ken *shot* the advancing Thompson in the chest.

More screams erupted from the crowd.

From the force of the advancement, Thompson fell forward onto Ken.

"He won't stop attacking!" Ken thought.

He shot and shot, as Thompson's heavy — *and unbeknownst to Ken*, already lifeless body leaned on him.

Smoke came out the other side of Thompson as Ken continued to shoot.

Then, Click. Click.

"My gun's empty," Ken realized as he and Thompson fell to the ground.

Pushing himself out from under Thompson, Ken half-crawled over to his partner.

Bill lay in the street, unable to get up.

"I need to get help!" Ken thought frantically.

Losing blood rapidly, and holding his throat shut with one hand, he quickly made his way to the police call box, sixty feet away. He pulled the handle, yelled his badge number, and followed with "Get help to 29th and Canal!"

Ken went back to Bill, and found him *unconscious*. He tried to stop the flow of blood. Meanwhile, he heard murmurs from the crowd—something about Bill's gun, and hiding any evidence. He searched Bill for his gun.

"It's missing!"

Dizzy from losing blood, Ken's head dropped, bringing the blood back to his head again. He reloaded his gun. Then, up onto his knees, he lifted his head, and pointed his revolver to the crowd shouting, "The next bastard who steps off that curb will be dead!"

Then Ken heard the sirens and saw red lights flashing from both directions. He was thankful, but also fearful. *"What if they don't recognize us in civilian clothes?"* They were plain-clothes officers that night.

Soon, he could see legs running from the squad cars and ambulances; and with one hand holding his throat together, and the other hand clasping his gun, Ken started shouting his badge number, "**1436...1436...1436!**"

The police understood.

Before he realized it, they were carrying him to the ambulance; and while they did so, Ken shouted, "Get the bitch in the green coat!"

After that, with great faith in his fellow officers, Ken allowed himself to relax, and he lost all consciousness.

Whew! It was exhausting just hearing all this. Ken had difficulty expressing himself, because he could hardly whisper. But Bill, although severely injured, was able to talk; and we kept turning to him for questions that could be answered.

We had *finally* learned the story!

I then asked, "What happened to the woman that pounded on Ken's head? Did they find her?"

Bill responded, "Yes, Shirley. Shortly thereafter, they found her hiding in a nearby car, and arrested her."

By now Ken and Bill were worn out, and so were we—and I am sure the nurse-nuns of Misericardia *[pronounced Miss-ah-CORD-ee-ah]* were, too. The injured had been brought to this hospital instead of County General, because it was the closest hospital available.

Misericordia wasn't used to all this attention. But they soon would be getting a lot of it—and loving it.

The history of Milwaukee's Misericordia Sisters begins with two French-Canadian nuns (Sister St. Celestin and Sister St. Fabian) of Montreal, Canada. In 1908, several local Milwaukee physicians made requests to Archbishop Sebastian G Messmer for the establishment of a new hospital in the city. The Misericordia Sisters were the immediate choice to lead this project. They arrived, and opened the Misericordia Hospital at 22nd and Juneau, where the Archbishop had been living (but he was being transferred to the Pabst mansion on Wisconsin Avenue). Later, the hospital moved to 22nd and Kilbourn.
www.wisconsinhistory.org/Records/Newspaper/BA11265

CHAPTER EIGHT

Mom, Dad, Mickey, and I left the hospital; and I suggested we stop at a little corner diner near our apartment, and have lunch. It was 11:00 a.m., and we could get a seat before the lunch crowd arrived. Mickey was excited when he heard me suggest that, because we *rarely* dined in a restaurant.

I parked near the front door, so Mom and Dad wouldn't have too far to walk. Mickey held his grandma's hand, jumping up and down. You would think he was going to the circus.

Papa Joe, behind the counter with his apron on, called out, "Welcome, folks! Grab a booth, and we'll be with you in a few minutes!"

We sat down, and the waitress soon dropped off the menus on her way to the kitchen. Papa Joe's was simply decorated. The walls were a cream color, and sparsely adorned with framed prints of Norman Rockwell paintings. The booths were in a maroon fake leather, and the counter had a glass case next to it with homemade pies to purchase—a slice, or take home a whole pie. The tabletops all had salt and pepper, catsup, and napkins on them.

I read the options on the menu to Mickey, and he finally chose Macaroni and Cheese (one of his favorite meals). I decided on an omelet, Mom chose a BLT, and Dad chose a hamburger. Mom also wanted a piece of pie, because she *loved* pies.

"How's our boy?" Dad asked as he pulled Mickey up onto his knee.

Mom added, "I have a story for you, Mickey...."

As Mom and Dad Stanelle fussed over Mickey, I began digging in my purse for something. I knew it would take about a half hour for our food to arrive, so I became lost in thought. I thought about how hard Ken had worked to complete the physical examination to become a police officer....

The physical examination was spelled out in a letter. Running a mile under ten minutes was only part of it. The 100-yard dash must be completed in less than fifteen seconds; and it went on and on about push-ups, chin-ups, sit-ups, hand-grip, etc.

Then there was his weight. According to the chart, at his height, *which was six foot,* he should be 190 pounds. I had Ken step on our scale, and he weighed in at 210. I looked at him, and promptly said, "You've got to diet and train."

Ken and I went to Sears, and I helped him pick out a cheap sweatsuit, socks, and tennis shoes. Every morning when he got home from working the night shift, we would drive out to the country, where I dropped him off; and then I would drive ahead one mile, park, and time him.

Mickey thought it was great fun — especially riding in the car. He watched for his dad; and when he could spot him coming down the lane, I would let him out of the car. He would jump up and down waving his arms excitedly. Peggy, dressed warm, and wrapped in a thick quilt, cooed happily.

We did this every day until we knew he could run the distance in the required time. The first day was rough; and when we got home, he could barely get up the stairs to the apartment. He just collapsed on the bed without a shower, pajamas, or a comment.

I couldn't resist teasing him, "Kinda out of shape, huh, pudgy?"

But then I gave him a hug, and added, "Heck, honey, it's only the first day."

The diet was another challenge. The first time I gave him his lunchbox, he could tell it felt light. He peeked inside, and exclaimed, "I'll starve to death!"

But deep down, I could tell he had a direction, and was determined to do this. It was a good thing his attitude changed, because this was a man who loved to eat. But even though Ken had this new direction, he felt he had to be secretive about the sparse lunch. The other guys surely would hoot and holler if they saw a measly grapefruit, when in the past he had a heavy lunchbox, *full* of food. He wanted to avoid the inevitable questions of why, why, etc. He didn't want to slip up, and let it out that he had applied for a job as a cop for the City of Milwaukee.

Later, at home, Ken was going to have his four ounce steak. I weighed it to be sure, and put it on his plate. He looked at me, and said, "You gotta be kidding!"

My one word to him was, "Eat."

He slowly cut the meat into tiny pieces, and chewed and chewed each mouthful to make it last longer.

On the Friday before his test, I woke him at noon. He was awake and dressed before he realized what time it was.

"How come you got me up so early?"

Casually I answered with, "You're going to do a light workout this afternoon, and you're not going to work tonight. I called you in sick."

"You what? You called me in sick when we need every dime we can get?"

"I thought of that, but the important thing is for you to pass that test, and you'll need every edge you can get…. Besides, you're as ready as you can be. Your weight has gone down to 194 — it looks like the rubber tire is almost gone. You can run the mile without trouble, and your 20 push-ups and 10 chin-ups are constant." I gave him a quick kiss, and added, "We can celebrate on those things alone!"

Saturday finally came, and I wished him good luck, and kissed him goodbye.

When he came home later, he looked a little worried, and then related the day's events. The practice in running paid off. He had felt strong, so he was sure he passed *that* part of it. He told about several men who wiped out on the running — maybe they took the curve too fast, or didn't run with their knees high enough.

Ken added, "The mile was the last test after the grueling 100-yard dash and the calisthenics. Some of the men had knots in their legs as tears streamed down their faces from the pain. One time, three men collided, and fell together. It turned out that one of the fallen men had broken a leg, and an ambulance was called!"

Ken did the mile in 6 minutes and 22 seconds.

****

The waitress brought us our food; and I came out of my thoughts, and back to reality. As we ate, I said, "I was thinking back to when Ken needed to prepare for his physical exam to become a police officer. He weighed in at 210 pounds, but a chart told us that for his height, he needed to weigh 190. He worked hard at it—exercising and dieting for almost three straight weeks. When he got on the scale, we saw that he had lost 16 pounds! *But,* he had lost so much in such a short time; it produced extra sugar in his blood. The doctor felt his arms, and said, 'You know, son…. You have such big bones; you should weigh more than the chart says. Your big frame could carry another 15 pounds easily. Go home, and put some weight on those bones, and get that sugar under control. See me next week.'"

Following his next appointment, Ken received a letter of congratulations from the Chief of Police, saying he would be sworn in as a Policeman on Monday, June 27, 1951 at 8:00 a.m.

Ken is in the top row, 4th from right.

Kenneth G. Stanelle, Milwaukee Policeman

Mom and Dad Stanelle enjoyed that memory; and after eating, when the waitress brought us our check, I said, "Now, I'm paying for this."

"You'll do nothing of the sort," Dad insisted, as he proceeded to hand money to the waitress.

I was secretly grateful. Ken and I lived on a strict budget, and when he would come home with his cashed check, we would go over the bills. I put the cash in various envelopes: one envelope for utilities and rent, one for gas for the Hudson, one for groceries, and last, but not least, $4.00 each month toward a vacation. That small amount would add up enough to enable us to rent a small cabin on a lake, where we could go fishing.

That *vacation* envelope got me thinking again as we walked to the car, got in, and Dad drove us home....

Chuck, one of Ken's hunting and fishing buddies, told him about some excellent fishing in the northern part of Wisconsin, right by Lake Superior. So, a few summers ago, instead of renting a cottage, we took the vacation savings, and spent it on gas instead, and headed north. We had an old rebuilt camper that provided beds when we opened it up, and we packed it with groceries and fishing equipment.

When we got to the little town of Cornucopia—*which wasn't much more than a crossroads with a general store*, Ken went into the store, and asked the owner where we could camp to do a little fishing.

He graciously said, "Well, if you back out the way you came in, watch for a road on your left with a small sign that says Siskiwit River. Turn left there, and you will find an opening in the trees on the right, just before the bridge. Follow that a little ways, and you should be able to find a place to park, and camp along the river."

We set up camp, and stayed the rest of the week. *Life was good.* Ken was camping and fishing.... What more could a man want? Besides, we had fish for breakfast *and* supper.

During the week, we visited the store again, and Ken, without asking *me* first, asked the owner if there was any land for sale.

Again, the owner surprised us, and said, "Well, I have ten acres I could sell you."

Oh boy, no sleep the next two nights! That's all Ken could talk about, and the land would cost us less than we paid for Freddy, our dog.

"Honey, we could have our own place, and I could build a hunting shack on it. If we could manage paying for Freddy, then...couldn't we manage another mountain?"

We looked at the designated spot, and I didn't see anything so special. It was just trees...but, it was on the road to town.

"Now how do you think we could afford lumber, and then get it up here?" I asked.

"You figure how we can budget to buy the land, and I'll figure how to get a hunting shack."

Then a big kiss and a big smile, and I knew he had me.

All of a sudden, Mom said, "Shirley, are you alright. I thought we lost you there for a minute."

I snapped to, and said, "Dad...I was in deep thought about the hunting shack at Lake Superior. I'll never forget how you pulled nails from that lumber."

Dad laughed, and said, "Well, *I'll* never forget that *either!* The Milwaukee law allowed you to give your building to someone if the other party tore it down, and took it away. That's how Ken got his lumber and window panes. A friend let him pile the wood on his lot, and several times I came down from Seymour, and pulled and straightened nails. When enough was gathered, Ken and I rented a truck, drove up there, and unloaded the lumber and nails onto the new land."

I blurted, "Ken and I were both excited about that shack—even though it didn't have electricity. Ken said that you and his best buddy, using a cross-cut saw, started on the big project."

Dad added, "That was a lot of hard work, but we had a hunting place that fall. I think five of Kenneth's friends came up to hunt!"

We arrived at the apartment, Dad parked our old Hudson by the back door, and I went in. I ran through the apartment, scooted out the front door, and hurried next door to pick up Peggy. I told Susie about Ken and Bill being in the same room, wrapped the blanket around Peggy, told Susie thank you, and hurried back to my apartment.

I got the folks settled in our bedroom, because they would be staying the night. We only had one bedroom, but our couch folded down, and made a bed good enough for me.

Mickey didn't want to take a nap, because *Grandma* and *Grandpa* were here, and he doesn't see them that much.

"Do you have some cards handy, Shirley? We'll play card games with him, and keep him company," Dad said.

Mom, added, "And, put the baby right next to me, so I can keep an eye on her at the same time."

"Don't you two want to take a nap?" I asked.

"Thanks, but we're fine. We would rather play with the children," Mom replied.

I found some regular playing cards, and also some children's cards that Mickey played with, and they all sat at the kitchen table.

While they were busy entertaining the children, I had time to think about supper. Then I remembered I had plenty of Thanksgiving leftovers, and I could just make up some more biscuits for short cake. We still had extra strawberry sauce and cream. If Ken and Bill had stopped, they would have eaten this.

I was glad the folks were here, even though they had to leave tomorrow. There was a big snowstorm coming in, and they wanted to leave right after seeing Ken one more time in the morning. *Besides*, all the relatives and friends back home were going to want to hear the details about the senseless fight. Mom and Dad being here, even for such a short time, helped me get adjusted to dealing with responsibilities by myself. They were having a good time at the table with Mickey, and I didn't want to disturb them, so I used a small counter in the pantry for mixing the biscuit dough.

While by myself, I started remembering a funny thing that happened about a year earlier when I answered the door to see Mom and Dad Stanelle standing there....

> They had decided to come down the 100 miles from Seymour, and surprise us. Normally that wouldn't faze me; but it was in the afternoon, and close to suppertime. I invited them in, and while they were taking their coats off, I ran to get Ken. He was outside doing something on the car, and I said, "Ken, honey, your folks are here."
>
> "Okay," he said, "I'll be right in."
>
> "But what am I going to do about supper? I made Venison Stroganoff, and your mother doesn't like venison—and we don't have anything else."
>
> "Just don't *tell* her," he casually stated.
>
> "But won't she realize it?"
>
> He then winked at me, and went into the house to greet them.
>
> That night I was a nervous wreck. I boiled the egg noodles, and served the *"Stroganoff,"* and I must say it was delicious.
>
> And what does my mother-in-law say?

"This is the *best* Stroganoff I have ever had. Would you mind sharing your recipe?"

I had used a recipe from a magazine I found several years before, but it used *beef*. We think Dad suspected, because he had a little grin on his face; and he knew from listening to Ken in the past that we ate everything we hunted…deer, moose, duck, quail, rabbit—and even squirrel. But he didn't say anything.

A year later, while visiting them, Mom stated, "I tried that Stroganoff recipe of yours, but it just didn't taste as good."

We never told her the truth, because she would have thought we were trying to fool her; but that wasn't it at all.

****

After supper and dishes, we all moved to the living room. The baby had her bottle while in Mom's arms, and we soon put her to bed. Mickey quickly pulled out his trucks and cars to roll on the floor. I excused myself, and hustled to the bedroom to put fresh sheets and pillowcases on the bed. The phone kept ringing all the while (as it did during supper). Luckily, there was a phone in the bedroom as well as in the kitchen. People from church were calling, and strangers too—all offering help in many ways…especially offering to babysit. I had a pad of paper by each phone, and jotted their names and phone numbers. I accepted several for that very week.

The television was on, and every station talked *only* about the police officers—the fight, how long they had been on the force, and where it happened. And, of course, we talked about it, too. It was nothing to laugh about, but we did bring up about Ken hitting that one guy out of his shoes. Dad said, "That must have been quite a powerhouse swing!"

I hadn't heard that saying since the comic books or TV westerns.

*****

Beyond dad's head, I saw our piano, and thought....

"My mother's piano."

My mother passed away when I was only eleven years old, and I inherited the piano. I carted it around whenever we moved. If you ever tried to move an upright piano, you had to know I really had a patient and strong husband.

When he was not singing *"Frankie & Johnnie,"* Ken would sit down, and play the piano by ear; and Mickey and I would dance when he would play the *"Boogie Woogie!"*

I turned my head from the piano, and stared at the picture of me in my wedding dress. It was long-sleeved, and made of taffeta; and it had a long train with ruffles. Buttons, covered with fabric, stretched up the bodice to the neck. I paid $39.00 for it.

"Mom, remember that dress?" I pointed to it. "You helped me pick it out. And then remember you made those darling little dresses for the two flower girls, so they would match my dress? Weren't they cute?"

Mom Stanelle and I enjoyed a relaxed and happy sigh.

It seemed like yesterday.

CHAPTER NINE

I woke Mickey, so he could get ready to go with us to the hospital; and then I picked up the baby, and changed her. I could hear the folks stirring. They would soon want breakfast. When I got out to the kitchen, Mom Stanelle was there; so I handed the baby to her, and proceeded to fix a bottle and make a pot of coffee.

Dad came to the kitchen, and sat at the table; and when Mickey came out, Mickey immediately jumped on his lap, and caused Dad to chuckle.

I didn't have any breakfast meats left in the refrigerator, and wouldn't be buying any until the next paycheck. I could make French toast, and that would only take two eggs, but still be filling. I always had bread on hand, because it was the main thing for Ken's lunchbox *and* for Peanut Butter-Jelly when Mickey got hungry between meals. There was a small bowl of strawberry sauce, left from last night. A little shake of powdered sugar on top of the toast with a spoonful of strawberries made the French toast special.

When we were finished eating, Dad held Peggy, while Mom did the few dishes, and I packed items for Peggy's visit to a new home this morning.

"Aren't you nervous about leaving the baby, Shirley?" Mom asked.

"Well, yes, but I can only have good thoughts about that. I need to be able to see Ken each day, and he needs to see me, too."

"I wish we lived closer, so I could take care of her."

"Thanks Mom, that would be nice; but it will all work out," I sort of mumbled *hoping* it would.

We all got in the Hudson, making our first stop to drop off the baby, just two blocks away; and then we were on our way to the hospital. I dropped everyone off at the door, drove to a parking spot, and hurried in. We punched number three for third floor, and when the door opened, Mickey ran out toward the room, which still had a policeman standing guard outside.

We learned that the police would continue to stand guard throughout the duration of Ken and Bill's hospital stay, due to death threats they had received.

The room was full of activity, and one nurse was checking Ken's vitals. Mickey didn't care. He quickly ran in, and jumped up on the bed—no longer afraid of the mummy.

I gave Ken a hug, kissed his fingertips, and then made room for his parents. Next, I went over to Bill's bed to say hello to Bill and to Helen. A nurse was changing the dressing on Bill's enormous wound. It didn't look right to her, and she was going to have the doctor look at it when he came in.

Meanwhile, Bill was telling us about the activity in the room the night before. Besides the reporters coming and taking their pictures, the detectives were in and out, and brought along their supplies. They had set up a small table after visiting hours, and brought glasses and an assortment of bottles of cheer. They were toasting the two patients, and cheering them on. Then they stashed it all in the bathroom. Bill was laughing, and Ken was nodding his head in agreement.

Then Ken wrote a note about a case he and Bill had worked on as *plain-clothes cops*. Bill read the note, and translated it: "When we had duty to check out a bar, we had to order bourbon to look like regular customers, and the bartender put two in front of us...."

Looking up, Bill said to us, "I don't touch the stuff, and Ken said he could never afford to buy it, so he wasn't a pro with drinking it, either.... But *someone* had to drink it!"

And there was laughter from Bill; and Ken was nodding with shoulders shaking.

Bill added laughingly, "So Ken would drink one down about halfway as fast as he could, and then switch the glasses, and sip on the other until we were ready to go. Ken had a rough time writing up his report that night."

****

The folks needed to go, and were pleased to see Ken sit up in bed, so he could give them a hug before they left. The doctor came in, and asked me if I could be there by 9:00 a.m. on Monday—just two days away. He was going to take off the bandages, and check on Ken's 281 stitches; and thought I should be there. I assured him I would be.

On the way home, I picked up Peggy, and everything was fine. I helped the folks get their belongings to their car, wished them a safe trip...

...and they were gone.

CHAPTER TEN

Monday morning found me pulling up to the hospital at 8:45, and hurrying in. I had dropped Peggy off to a sitter, Mickey off to kindergarten, and couldn't arrive any sooner. I didn't want to be late. When I got to the room, the hospital attendants had just entered with their dolly. They were going to transfer Ken to it. After giving Ken a quick hug, I stepped aside to let them move him out of the room, and then I followed them.

The room they took him to had one bed, some hospital equipment, and a few chairs. After they transferred him to that bed, I stood at the end of it, where I could watch, and still be out of the doctor's way.

The doctor came in, and sat down next to Ken. He quietly proceeded to unwind the gauze. Round and round and round—taking what seemed like *forever!* Finally, it was all off, and Ken was watching every move or twitch in my face and eyes.

He always said I did not have a poker face. He always knew, or thought he knew, what I was thinking.

"Oh my God.... My beautiful husband's face.... What did they do to him?" I thought. But I tried really hard not to let Ken see my dismay.

Then the doctor handed him a mirror. I witnessed something so unbelievable as I watched Ken. In slow motion, his face started to turn ghostly white from the top of his head down to his chin.

Ken turned away from the mirror, and the doctor had a pan ready for him to throw up in.

The doctor knew.

I rushed to Ken's side, and held him as he wept, and I wept.

The doctor gave us a few minutes, and then he started his examination. The stitches ran from about two inches above Ken's ear, down to his chin. It also took a detour toward his throat. The stitches showed where they put his ear back on. Ken's face was black and blue, and very swollen. Some stitches were inside his mouth, as well; because his saliva gland had been pierced, and would no longer be able to function. The knife had stopped just short of cutting his juggler.

The doctor then examined the back of Ken's head, and that is when he discovered dried blood and a concussion that had not been treated. Ken's head and face were so full of blood when he arrived at the hospital that the only concern they had was to get his face back together, and the rest was evidently overlooked. The doctor surmised from the story that the woman who was hitting Ken with the steel-plated, size-13 shoe did the damage, until Ken stopped her with a backhanded swipe.

That concussion would eventually cost him his beloved job.

****

The doctor and nurse re-bandaged Ken using a thick amount of heavy gauze on the left side of his face, covering the stitches. They held it on with a long Ace bandage that wrapped around his chin and over his head, but leaving the rest of his face exposed. When the doctor was finished, the hospital attendants came in, and transferred him to the dolly again; and I walked alongside him holding his hand.

When we entered the room, Bill cheered, "Hey, buddy, now we can see that ugly face of yours again!"

Ken's eyes just twinkled, and he wrote on his paper, "Cigarette.... Cigarette!"

Ken's mouth was still wired, so he still couldn't eat or talk; but he could have his cigarette.

The doctors told Ken, sadly, that he would never drink out of a cup, or walk without crutches. Of course, Ken was determined to *prove them wrong.*

After he returned to his bed, Sister Immaculate Heart of Mary moved his bed over next to Bill's for the benefit of a photographer; and Bill lit the cigarette for him. Sister Mary was in the room overseeing the nurse treating Bill.

The doctor had agreed earlier that there was something stopping the healing of Bill's leg. Every day, for days, the cut would have to be reopened, and then searched for a hidden *"something that must be there."*

The cut eventually became over two inches wide before they found the piece of wool yarn from the pants Bill wore the night he was attacked.

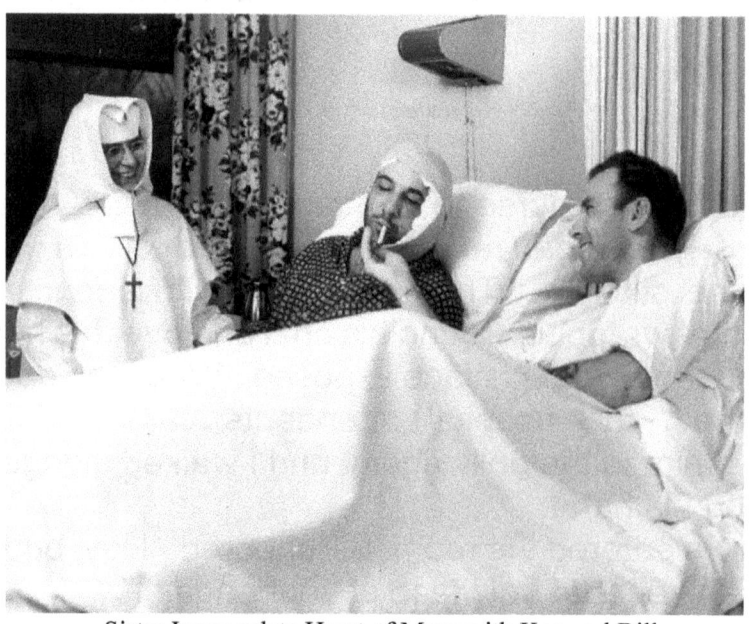

Sister Immaculate Heart of Mary with Ken and Bill

CHAPTER ELEVEN

It was two weeks before Ken could have anything but liquid from a straw. The diet consisted of Jell-O, beverages, broth, or pureed food. His jaw was still wired, and he still couldn't talk normally…just whisper. But that didn't keep Ken down! He became proficient at writing his thoughts, and that began a series of *ditties:*

At noon, there was always a little poem waiting for the Sisters when they picked up the menu cards. Here are four samples of Ken's little ditties—written to bring on a smile:

Thirty-eight days in this wonderful place,
And the end is not in sight.
An X goes on the calendar
We mark it every night.
We're not complaining, we like it here,
We're quiet as a mouse.
The only way we'll leave this place,
Is when they throw us out.

There were no poems for a couple of days,
We both were very busy.
With needles and pills and sheets and chills,
It almost made us dizzy.
Of course, from us you'll never hear,
A complaint or grief to you,
With beans, tomatoes, and mashed potatoes,
I'm sure we'll live, don't you?

When your recovery is complete,
I'll take you out to dine.
I answered him, and plainly said,
The treat will be all mine.
I'll bring you back to this hospital,

Where the food is really fine.

    People ask us how we feel,
With Christmas drawing near.
    In a hospital, sick with aches and pains,
And still so full of cheer
    The secret is, I'll tell you now,
You'll be the first to know.
    With delicious food, and a comfortable bed,
And the ceiling full of mistletoe.

One day when I went to his room to visit, and there was no one there. I panicked for a moment when I realized that Bill was gone, too. So I went to the nurses' station, and asked—fearing that Ken had had a setback.

But the nurse laughed, and said, "Oh they may be as far as Room 315 by now."

I looked at her quizzically, and she laughed again saying, "Go see for *yourself.*"

I hurried down the hall, and there they were—visiting!

Ken decided to wheel Bill around, and visit the other patients. Ken could walk, and Bill could talk. They did this every day for the rest of their time in the hospital. The stops depended on how sick the patient was. Sometimes it was just a wave and good morning; other times it was a real visit. But once they had started their rounds, the patients looked forward to their stop.

Sometimes a nurse would ask them to see Room *such and such,* because the person in that room was very depressed. The Sisters gave Ken and Bill leeway to do as they pleased.

These two guest officers brought **life** into the hospital. The patients enjoyed it, and the Sisters enjoyed it, too.

CHAPTER TWELVE

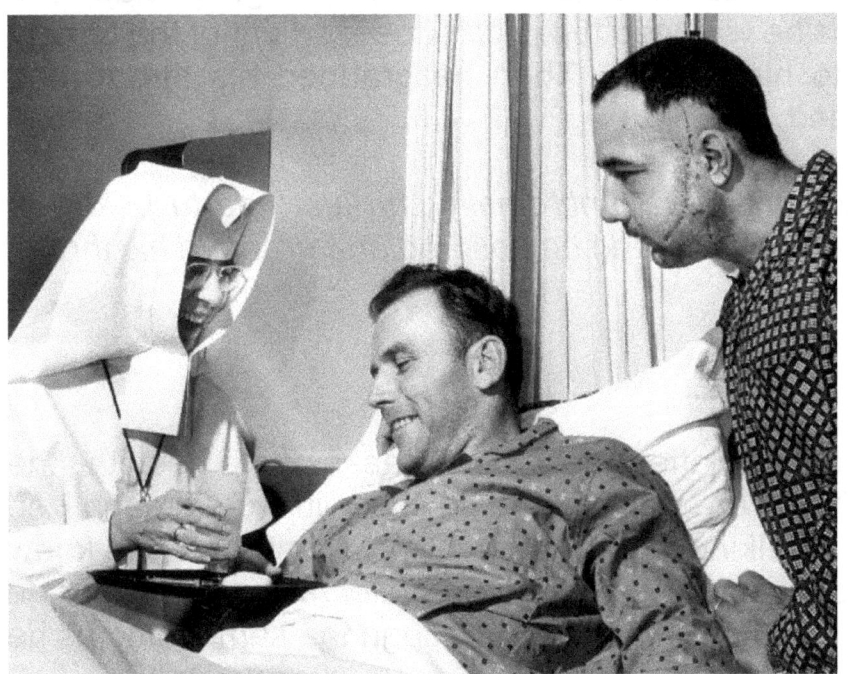

Sister Immaculate Heart of Mary with Ken and Bill

As the days flowed by slowly, both men began to feel stronger. Therapy had begun on Bill's leg as soon as the piece of wool yarn was removed; and once Ken's mouth was unwired, he underwent shock therapy. Small tabs, or electrodes, were attached to Ken's head and neck, and this treatment was used to stimulate his brain.

One of the nuns assigned to Ken's care was Sister Max. She was assigned the task of getting Ken's salivary glands to function again. There are three major pairs of salivary glands in the mouth—the largest pair of glands is called the parotid. All three glands produce saliva, and it was Nurse Max's job to strengthen the one and only gland not injured, so it could produce enough saliva by itself.

The first day she arrived, her only tool was a lemon. Standing near Ken as he lay in his bed, she cut the lemon in two, and started squeezing. His eyes grew wider and wider as he watched the juice squeezed out of the lemon, and into his mouth. Then he grabbed his throat, and screamed.

This was the ritual until finally she just had to poke her head in the room, and he hollered and grabbed his throat.

****

One night, after a few more weeks at the hospital, the detectives were visiting, and having a little cheer; and Ken felt up to talking. He missed telling the stories. He knew the detectives experienced the *observance class*, and he wanted to know if they went through the same thing as he did.

"Hey, did you guys have Sgt. Scharp? Did *you* Bill? He used to preach over and over that *observation* to the policeman is what the *heart* is to the *human body*....

> "It started with license plates. *I concentrated so hard that I bet I could out-guess you guys.* He'd take a stack of plates, and flash them in front of you. Then he asked to have them written down. At first I was lucky to get two numbers, and then the Sergeant explained, 'When you spot a license plate in a flash as I'm doing, close your eyes immediately, and picture that glimpse in your mind until it's like an instant replay on TV.'
>
> "Each day, whenever we had a few minutes between classes, we would play License Plate Replay. It really got to be a lot of fun."

Ken went into Sergeant Scharp's voice—trying to sound like him again:

"'However, license plates are only a small part of the observation game.... Never sit in a public building with your back to a door; always be in a position to observe. Learn makes and models of cars. Check them out as you walk the streets, and play a game with yourself: As you walk a block, see how close you have to get to a parked car before you can identify its year, make, and model. Look in used car lots and new car showrooms until recognizing a car is second nature to you.'"

Following Ken's imitation, there was cheering and hollering in the room; and someone quickly closed the door while Ken continued.

"The Sarge would flash colored slides of cars on a screen, and we would call out the make, model and year. Like, '52 blue Chevy Tudor' or '53 maroon Chrysler Sedan.'

"I even had my family in on the game. When we were in the car, we called out license plate numbers. Shirley got pretty good, and now recognizes makes of cars.

"Besides memorizing car descriptions, we had to learn to memorize what people looked like. We soon learned to describe someone with a Roman nose, a receding hairline, a protruding Adam's apple, etc.

"My son, Mickey, would excel at this; and sometimes it was embarrassing: 'Dad! Look! That guy has an Adam's apple!'

"It was okay when we were safely past someone walking on the street; but that time, he pointed out someone near us in the store, and I felt like burying my head...."

"I was soon to learn it was never over. The day started in class like any other, and there was absolutely no warning or premonition of what was about to happen....

"It was the second hour, and the Sarge was getting his books lined up on his desk to start the class when a man came in. He walked quietly across the stage, and laid some papers in front of the Sarge.

"The man said, 'Excuse me, Sgt. Scharf, but you are to sign these.... They're from upstairs.'

"Now, everyone knew that *'upstairs'* meant the *Chief's* office, so it was plain where the papers originated. Sgt. Scharf scanned them over one by one, and said, 'Dave, I signed these yesterday.'

"'Maybe you did Sarge, but I got orders for you to sign them.'

"'Look, Dave, I don't care about your orders. They were signed yesterday.... What the hell's going on upstairs? Don't they know what's going on?'

"Dave fumbled for words, and said, 'Sorry Sarge. I just follow orders....'"

"We could all see it was embarrassing for the Sarge, and *some* scrunched down in their seats. The Sergeant glanced at the sea of faces in front of him, and said evenly, 'Alright, Dave, I'll sign them again; but I'll see you upstairs right after class.'

"Sgt. Scharf scribbled across the pages, and shoved them impatiently at Dave, who picked them up, and walked quickly from the room.

"It was very quiet, and the Sergeant seemed to have difficulty getting his wits about him.

"'Alright, men, page 34 in *Arrest, Search and Seizure.*'

"A rustle of books filled the room; and after a few seconds, it was quiet again. The Sarge sat quietly, and I couldn't help but think to myself that I had never seen the Sergeant angry, and it was just not like him. Quietly he said, 'On second thought, men, take out your pencils and paper.'

"We did as we were told, and again it turned quiet.

"'Now,' the Sergeant said with a grin on his face, 'Write down a complete description of the man who was just in here!'

"A shocked silence hit us all; and we all bent our heads, and started writing.

"I wrote 'White Caucasian, about 5'10", black hair, black glasses....' Or was it brown glasses? *Damn!* Not sure blue coat or grey. *Damn again!*, as I searched my mind for the answers.

I worked laboriously; and erasers were really flying all around me as everyone else also struggled with the description.

"Suddenly, the Sergeant said, 'Time's up! You've had enough time to write a letter home to mother. Pass them to the aisle; and Williams, you bring them up here.'

One of the detectives in the hospital room interrupted Ken to say, "Boy, the Sergeant was a damned good actor, wasn't he?"

Ken nodded, and continued his story....

"As the papers were gathered, the Sarge went to the blackboard, and wrote:

> White male, Caucasian, 5'11" tall, about forty years-old, brown hair, blue eyes, gold-rimmed glasses, ruddy complexion, blue sport coat, gray pants, white shirt, maroon tie, black shoes, name Dave.

"The papers were laid on the desk. The Sergeant picked up the stack, and said, 'On the blackboard is the *correct* description of Dave who was in here ten minutes ago. I am now going to read *yours*.'

"'White Caucasian, 5'9", black hair, gray sport coat, white shirt.'

"The Sarge looked up, and said, 'Didn't Dave have any pants? Was Dave a male or a female?'

"A snicker of laughter rippled through the room.

"The paper was dropped in the wastebasket, and the Sarge read another.

'Male *Caukshion* — what the hell is a *Caukshion?*, brown eyes, blue suit and tie.

'How the hell can you see brown eyes, and miss the coat and pants?'

"The more the Sarge read, the funnier it got, and the room roared with laughter...."

Ken laughed and said, "You know, guys, this would be a great subject for a stand-up comedian."

One of the detectives exclaimed, "You're making the story funny yourself, Stanelle!"
Ken smiled, and continued….

"Finally, the funny part ended. The Sergeant had laughed with us, and suddenly it was quiet. Then he firmly stated, 'And your sister or brother could be killed and *you*… **YOU!**' he roared, 'wouldn't be able to give a description!'

"The Sergeant snapped, 'So DAMNED FUNNY! It's so funny that had Dave stabbed me in the back, and got away, sixty-four men would not have been able to give an accurate description of him! It's so goddamn funny for the assailant! Well, DAMMIT, it's NOT FUNNY!!'"

Ken then explained, "You could have heard a mosquito fart in the room as the words sunk home.

'You want to be policemen?' Sergeant Scharf went on, 'then you better start acting like one. You will observe, observe, **OBSERVE!**' he bellowed."

Ken's imitation, and the laughing became too noisy. So at this point, a nun stuck her head in the door, and put her finger to her lips, indicating her request to be quiet.

Ken nodded respectfully, and in a quieter tone, he finished his story:

"I don't know about you fellows, but that afternoon as I walked to the parking lot, I wasn't exhausted; I was scared – spooked by what the Sergeant said…and I *observed*. I stared at every person I saw on the street. I tried to have eyes in back of my head, and I damn near ran into the hood of a car, I was looking around so much.

"Usually when I get home, I tell Shirley about my day, but that night I couldn't think of anything to tell her. I had gotten drummed into me the most important lesson I ever had by a man who I respected…. And as I closed my eyes to sleep, I vowed I would *never* get caught like that again. I strive to be the best observation man alive."

Ken paused, and then added, "I only have one exception….
I wish I had never observed last Thanksgiving night."

CHAPTER THIRTEEN

My days fell into a schedule with the mornings all the same. Every day, the first thing I did before either of the children woke was to take our dog, Freddy, out for a quick walk. The poor guy didn't know what was wrong, with Ken still being in the hospital. His master was gone.

I know, you are probably wondering what we were doing with a huge dog in a city *and* low income....

One day before we moved to Milwaukee, Ken came to me, and said, "Come with me. I want you to see something."

"For how long?"

"Not long...it's only about 20 miles from here. Grab Mickey, and let's go."

So off we went; and 30 minutes later, we pulled into a large driveway in front of what looked like a possible farm.

"What is this place?" I asked. We walked around the back, and then I saw the kennel with lots of Labradors. Ken led me to one, and the Lab bounded up and down when he saw him. I know I had a great big question mark sitting on top of my head, and Ken started to explain when George came walking around the corner of the kennel.

"Hey, Ken. I see you brought the little lady with you, and is this your little boy?"

"Yup, this is Shirley and Mickey. All future duck hunters!"

"That's how he found this place," I thought. *"His hunting friends must have told him about it."*

Ken said to me, "This is only the third time I've been here; and *this* boy connected with me, and me with him...." Turning to George, he continued, "Tell her, George, about his lineage."

George smiled, and proudly said, "His father was a National Field Dog Trial winner!"

I knew a little bit of what they were talking about, because we went to a Field Trial competition one time just to watch.

"How much is he?" Ken asked.

"We're letting him go for $250.00." Then George started explaining how wonderful Labradors are with children.

Tactfully, Ken responded, "Thanks, George. It's something we'll think about, and talk about."

"Sure thing! Just stop by anytime," George answered.

We returned to the car, and began driving home. I looked at Ken with the same question mark sitting on the top of my head.

When we were home sitting at the kitchen table with a cup of coffee to sip on, he told me how he happened to get acquainted with the Lab.... Then he asked, "Could we have a dog?"

I wasn't surprised that he would ask that question.
I wasn't born yesterday.

My answer was immediate, "You know we can't afford it."

"I know, but can we go over our finances, and see what we *can* afford? Maybe he'll come down a little."

"Right now, we can afford $25.00," I stated. I hadn't said if I liked the dog or not...*or* if we should even *have* a dog or not; but Ken jumped up out of his seat, pulled me up, and said, "I love you, honey. I'll talk to George in a few days...."

A few days later, Ken bounded into the kitchen, and said, "Let's talk again! I talked with George, and he is willing to let us pay him $25.00 a month until the full price is paid...*but* we have to leave him there until he is paid for. What do you think?"

I swear. He was like a little kid at Christmas-time.

Ken made the deal, and we decided on a name for him. It would be Frederick, or Freddy for short.

When Ken told his dad that we bought a dog, he immediately asked, "How much?"

"Twenty-five dollars," answered Ken without telling him the rest of the story—that it would be $25 each month for *10 months.*

"Twenty-five dollars!" he yelled. "Are you crazy, boy? The dang animal will eat you out of house and home."

His dad just shook his head, and walked away.

Ken never grew up with a dog or house pet. The dogs, if there were any, stayed outside....
Anyhow, that is how we acquired Freddy.

Freddy

****

Each day, while Ken was in the hospital, Freddy look at me frantically, *"Let's go! Let's go!"*

"*Okay, okay!*" I would say as I grabbed his leash, and we went outside. As I walked with him, I would think about the comfort he gave the whole family while we had him. He was so good with the children; and turned out, he was a natural field dog champion in his own right. We just never wasted money on booze, clothes, and nightlife. Freddy was worth every penny we spent. We kept saving extra pennies, and shortened the time to five months instead of the ten.

Anyhow, after Freddy's walk, my day continued with getting Peggy ready to go to a sitter, Mickey to school, and myself to the hospital to see Ken. Afterwards, I would reverse that operation, and we were home for the afternoon.

I wondered how I would be able to last without Ken.

****

Breaking the monotony of these days, Joe, a friend of Ken's, stopped by our home to learn the latest news on him. Ken used to moonlight for him—painting houses for extra cash. I kept trying to keep Joe there, giving him coffee and cookies, just to have an adult conversation. He could never stay long, because he had a crew working during the days. He could just stop by, and check on Ken's progress with me during the weekdays—and at the *hospital,* visit with Ken on Sundays.

Once, we were talking about Ken's storytelling, and the conversation led to the time when Ken was a beat cop. By the time we both finished relating the story, we were in tears laughing. The story was about a beat cop who observed something while walking in an alley.

I knew the story because Ken told it many times, and friends would be rolling on the floor laughing. I filled in when Joe would miss a point:

Molly worked at a bar, and sometimes stayed after hours, and came home loaded. She lived alone, and had an apartment with windows right next to the alley. When she came home late in that condition, she took off her shirt and bra, got on her knees, and scrubbed the floor. She was well endowed, so you can imagine what would go swinging.

Anyone walking the alley would be able to see this action. To see better, there was a wooden fence next to the alley; and if climbed, it made it even easier to see. *So,* the beat cop decided to share his find; and one evening, when Molly came home ready to scrub, four or five other city renowned officers joined him. There they were, with badges covered and hat brims drawn down, enjoying the scene.... Until all of a sudden, with a loud creak, the fence broke with their weights.

Picture the scene of the Keystone Kops...*running.*

A neighbor called in a disturbance, a motorcycle cop jumped on his bike – *and ran into a telephone pole;* and one of the cops casually walked up to the house that called in the disturbance to ask how he could be of help.

The neighbor praised the cop for his quick service!

CHAPTER FOURTEEN

Christmas was coming, and Mickey was getting all excited about Santa Claus. I tried to do the things we normally did when Ken was there—like driving the Hudson around to see the Christmas trimmings; and one day we drove to a tree place, and found a tree that I could handle.

Mickey excitedly helped me bring up the decorations from the basement, and together we did the decorating. Peggy and Freddy watched in amazement—especially when we turned on all the lights, and Mickey and I danced around the tree. That happiness helped me.

Christmas shopping was a little harder—controlling Mickey and pushing Peggy in a cart at the same time. But when it got too hard, I would just call it a day, and we would go home.

Sometimes in the morning, I would leave the hospital an hour earlier to shop for Mickey's gifts—from us *and* from Santa (Ken wanted me to get Mickey a big fire truck). I would take the gifts home, and hide them before I picked up Mickey and Peggy.

It helped having a responsibility to keep me going. It also helped me later in life to know to keep busy when things turned down. Hard work is the best medicine, because one has no time to think or feel the pain.

****

The afternoons were all about the children and our dog. Sometimes we all bundled up in the car, and I drove out to the country, where I could let Freddy out, and he could run. I carried Peggy, while Mickey ran after Freddy. It was cold, but we didn't care. Sometimes just a walk around the block with Peggy in her carriage,

Freddy on a leash, and Mickey skipping on ahead, helped pass the day.

On the weekends, Mickey would go to the hospital with me. One time, he had something he made for his daddy. It was a page from a coloring book, entitled "Real Pals." A horse was nuzzling a big dog. Mickey colored both animals brown—quite nicely, keeping in the lines. On the top, he wrote, "To Daddy, From Mickey."

We hung it up in Ken's hospital room, and Ken was proud to show everyone what his son did; Mickey was proud to see it on display.

Ken felt bad for me. Every morning I would tell him everything we did, and he would try to give us suggestions of more things we could do. As December 25th was getting closer, and no sign of Ken getting out of the hospital, I worried about how we would celebrate. I knew I could go to church with the children on Christmas Eve, and everyone would be kind to us, as they always were each Sunday.

As I think back, I don't know how people handle tragedies without a church-family's support.

CHAPTER FIFTEEN

A week before Christmas during my daily visit, I was informed, happily, that the nuns had a meeting, and decided that our families should be allowed to use the lobby for a Christmas celebration. There was a huge, decorated tree in one corner, and we could make it our own.

Ken and Bill were brought down in their pajamas and robes, and our families were all together. Ken's bandages were off, and Bill was still in a wheelchair; but they got in the spirit—just happy they could enjoy Christmas with the family. The press was informed; and they arrived, also.

Helen and I planned a small menu of holiday foods that we could enjoy after the presents. We would have dinner-roll sandwiches with ham & cheese; a platter of pickles, olives, and grape tomatoes; chips & dip; a cake—and of course, Christmas cookies.

Gathering together on Christmas Eve was exciting. Helen and I and the children were all dressed up in our Christmas clothes. I didn't want to spend money to buy anything, and I didn't need to because my white felt skirt (with a full swing) and a red top made it festive. Mickey had a white shirt with cufflinks, and it was easy to find a pretty dress for Peggy.

A patrol officer was assigned to us to help unload our cars. I pulled up to the main door, and he met us just like at a fancy hotel. He unloaded the presents and food, and parked the car. He did the same when Helen arrived with sons, William and Scott—and also Mrs. Clara Kasten, Bill's mother.

There were so many packages to open that little William and Mickey had to help their dads. The guys received some forty packages, including gifts from fellow officers at the Third Precinct, and also from Chief Howard O. Johnson. Of course, there were cigarettes for Ken; ties for when they would be plain-clothes officers again; candies & dried fruit; and an assortment of funny gifts.

Ken had written a Christmas prayer/poem, and I had it printed on nice paper. He gave it to the Kastens and to the Sisters:

A CHRISTMAS PRAYER

On Christmas day so long ago,
*   The Christ child came to Earth.*
That wondrous day in Bethlehem,
*   We celebrate his birth.*
And since that day, it's plain to see,
*   That He is everywhere.*
So with that thought I offer Him,

This humble little prayer:
We thank thee Father for our lives,
*   You spared with loving hands,*
For reasons known to only You,
*   I think we understand.*
Things left to do, more hills to climb,
*   For things on Earth undone.*
We ask thee Father, with all our hearts,
*   The courage for things to come.*
And so I close this little prayer,
*   With this final thought in mind,*
We thank thee Father for sparing us,
*   Thy kingdom yet to find.*

Amen

KGS

We were all enjoying the evening, and Mickey was playing with his fire truck, when the nuns surprised us again. They joined us in all their finery, and sang to us the following song:

To Our Dear Patients, Kasten & Stanelle
written by
Sister Immaculate Heart of Mary
Misericordia Hospital
Sung to the tune of *"Funiculì, Funiculà"*

Misericordia is glad to have you
This is no lie! This is no lie!

With happy and jolly fellers like you two
Days are not dry! Days are not dry!
With laugh, and song, and jokes the day soon passes
Full soon is gone! Full soon is gone!
For mirth was made for young lads and lasses
That's far from wrong! That's far from wrong!

CHORUS
Harken! Harken!
Life is worth living
Harken! Harken!
Life is worth living
Tra la la la, tra la la la, tra la
Don't you folks agree?
Tra la la la, tra la la la!

Some think the world is made for fun and frolic
And so do you! And so do you!
Some think it well to be all melancholic
Yes, some folks do! Yes, some folks do!
You, you love to spend your time in joking
With everyone! With everyone!
There is always time for good merrymaking
It's lots of fun! It's lots of fun!

CHORUS
Keep up! Keep up!
We enjoy you here
Keep up! Keep up!
We enjoy you here
Tra la la la, tra la la la, tra la la!

*Daily the hospital sees you meandering
On all the floors! On all the floors!
A great number of good friends you are making
At every door! At every door!
Your kind words, a wink, a smile or your laughter
Spend lavishly! Spend lavishly!
Make each and everyone feel so much better
Immediately! Immediately!*

*CHORUS
Bravo! Bravo!
The world seems brighter
Bravo! Bravo!
The world seems brighter
Tra la la la, tra la la la, tra la la la!
When you are around!
Tra la la la, tra la la la tra la la la!*

It truly was a Christmas we would never forget.

CHAPTER SIXTEEN

Ken was getting stronger every day, and would take long walks around the hospital corridors investigating. Most mornings, we would take a walk *together*, and he would tell me something he had heard, or some little *juicy-secret*. One day it affected us—it surprised and saddened me.

"You know Bob and Marge?"

"Yeah, what about 'em?"

"Well, they're gone," he replied.

"Gone...what do you mean by *gone?*"

Bob was a policeman, and Ken met him when he was a beat cop. We would go to each other's homes, and play cards. Their son was the same age as Mickey, and they played while we visited. Peggy stayed near us.

"Well," Ken replied, "Bob was arrested.... He was caught being a *Peeping Tom*...and there were the *other* instances against him. Marge was so distressed and humiliated that she and their boy left for Missouri, where she has friends. Bob had to leave the Department, and I guess he'll go down to Missouri, too. I understand they just left without contacting anyone."

That was disturbing news, but I quickly got over it when we rounded another corner....

Ken showed me another place he discovered. I loved it. We could walk arm in arm; and have a hug or embrace around this or that corner. This was something I *really missed*, and he did, too.

One day, back in his room, Ken told Bill to pull his curtains, so I could crawl in bed with him. Of course, *that* would never work. Another day, while walking, we came to St. Patrick's Hall. We entered through a back entrance, where there were dividers in a row, draperies hanging from various holders, and other chairs and furniture.

"I've been checking this place out for a week. It's used on certain days, and today is not one of them," Ken said with a big smile.

Pulling a few old drapes off the hangers, he placed them down on a hidden spot on the floor, and pulled me down to the floor with him.

When we got back in the room, Ken looked at Bill with a grin on his face like a Cheshire Cat.

My man may have been recovering, but he wasn't dead yet!

CHAPTER SEVENTEEN

The Milwaukee Public, which kept a close eye on the recoveries, found out that the City was not going to pay for Ken's plastic surgery. They were outraged. The Police Department and City Hall were bombarded with letters and phone calls. The Public won. The City would pay for the necessary operation and hospital stay, and a date was set for the end of the year (December of 1958) at Mount Sinai Hospital of Milwaukee.

****

Meanwhile, I had excitement of my own at the apartment house. The tenant from the third floor came down, and asked if I would be home that evening. She had hired the ten-year-old neighbor girl to babysit while they went out; but was hoping for an adult to be around.

Around nine that evening, the little girl came down the back stairs, and asked if I would help her, because the baby just woke up. My two children were both sleeping; so I followed her up. I started looking for a kettle to warm the baby bottle. I first looked in the oven, and then in the cupboard, where I found it.

I wanted to scream, but couldn't because I would have frightened the girl. The oven and the cupboards were moving. They were full of *cockroaches!* I got brave, and put on the kettle of water; and when the baby was settled, I returned downstairs. It was too late for me to call Ken, and cry to him; so I had to wait until morning.

The next day, I first called the exterminator, then the landlord, and finally started to look for another place to live.

The tenants were migratory, and had brought the nasty insects with them from Down South. It's possible that some people don't seem to mind cockroaches too much, but my only experience before this was seeing them in a book.

Later that morning, Ken felt bad for me as I was telling him my tale of woe, and he couldn't be there to help me. Our friends, Roberta and Ed Gensch, knew of a real estate agent, and we started looking. After a few days of hunting, we settled on a little Cape Cod (a one-story home with slanted roof and dormers) at the outskirts of the city. The price of the house was $16,400, and Ken qualified for a VA loan at 4%.

****

Finally, almost three months after the fight that landed both Ken and Bill in the hospital, the doctors decided they could finish recuperating at home. I was very happy to go, and pick up Ken. As the attendants at the hospital got him in the car, I excitedly said, "I'll show you the house, and you can see if you like it!"

When you've been in the hospital a long time, and finally get to go home, it hits you; and the fresh air almost knocks you out.

Well, after looking at the house, Ken was ready to drop, so he says, "O.K. *we'll, buy it; we'll buy it!* Just get me home to bed!"

We got home, and I started packing boxes. I was afraid the cockroaches would move down to our apartment before we had a chance to get out of there. Most nights, I would wake with a start, and with bare feet, creep to the kitchen pantry, reach around the door frame, and click on the light.

Never did see any more cockroaches, but my skin crawled every time I thought of them.

CHAPTER EIGHTEEN

In March of 1958, Ken's buddies at the precinct moved us into our Cape Cod; and daily, the house became full of cops—just shooting *"the bull."* One day, Harold and Vern stopped in. They were scheduled to begin Training School that weekend. That prompted Ken to ask, "If you'd like, I can give you a few pointers."

Harold and Vern appeared eager, so Ken began....

"First you need to contemplate how the Safety Building is laid out. The 2nd floor is actually the third floor, because of the sloping terrain. Entering from the State Street side, you only have two short flights of stairs to the classroom. From the front of the building, you have three floors to climb. It only took one trip to convince me to park in back, and enter from the State Street side.

"The front of the building has another problem. Training Class starts at the same time as the police are changing shifts. The courts, City Attorney, and D.A.'s offices are also located at the front. In short, it is one helluva busy place, so all of us trainees would converge on the back side of the building to keep out of the way.

"Once inside, it is a short walk down the marble hall to the classroom itself. It's a simple room that is long and narrow with rows of chairs that have wide writing arms on them. The end of the room has a raised section like a stage with a plain wooden rostrum on one side, and a simple table and chair on the other. On that table, when I first walked in, there was a plain two-cell, metal flashlight with a bullet hole in the front, and the torn metal where it made its exit out the back. I wondered if I would ever learn about the cop or criminal who held it. This clean simplicity was to be my place of study for the next eight weeks.

"To explain each day in the classroom is beyond my memory's capabilities; but certain things stand out, and made a lasting impression on me. The first was report-writing, in which I immediately found out how bad at writing I was. A simple spelling test was given. Words like *courtesy, judicial, memorandum, accident*, etc. were used in the one hundred-word test. Sgt. Scharf was the instructor, and he simply told us we could have no more than ten wrong, if we wanted to pass. I remember while taking the test, I could see my high school teacher. I wished I had studied harder.

"I came out with eight wrong, and passed the test. Sgt. Scharf, with his half-smile, told us, 'Those of you who failed will take a special spelling class for thirty minutes *each day for a week* after regular class. The rest of you need not come unless you want to.'"

Ken briefly stopped his storytelling to say, "So don't screw up you guys…. Want a beer?"

The guys nodded, Ken grabbed them each a beer, and then continued.

"One guy…*I don't remember his name*, raised his hand, and asked 'Sir, why the spelling bit in the training school?' Sgt. Scharf answered, 'If you hand in an accident report, or a report of any kind that has a misspelling in its contents, the Precinct Commander will give it back to you to re-do. All reports must and will have proper spelling!'

"I tell you what guys…. I signed up for the spelling class voluntarily. You will probably feel this way too—a spelling class when all you want to do is be a cop?

"Hey Shirl! Do we have some chips left?"

I was giggling to myself as I overheard him tell these two rookies—who were incidentally eating it up…. He told story after story. This was good for him to tell the stories to someone else besides me.

I left the bowl of chips on the coffee table, and scooted out so he could continue.

"Each day was different except for one thing—City Ordinances. We always got at least an hour or two a day on those stupid ordinances, and there was no escape. We all quickly learned to hate them! But they were a necessary evil; as I found out later—very, very useful to know.

"I think it was the third day of class that we were told we would be visiting the morgue. They took us down in groups of ten with Sgt. Scharf as our guide—our feet making noises on the stairs. We entered the room with the plain sign that said 'MORGUE.' It isn't much, with a row of drawers along one wall, and a refrigerated glass case on the other. There's a plain table and a floor drain with large lights above it that I figured was where the autopsies were conducted.

"The man in charge was in his 50's, with glasses and a bald head. He wore a white coat; and I mentally chuckled, and asked myself, *'For who? You'd think they would wear maroon or red coats, as their job could be a messy one.'* His name was Dr. Swift. I wonder if he'll still be there to guide you?

"Anyway, Dr. Swift went on to tell about the morgue's inhabitants. Oftentimes they have bodies that are in themselves evidence; and it's his job to confirm, through a strict, ritualistic procedure, the cause of death—regardless of the obvious signs.

"For example, he told us, 'A murder case came out of our autopsy that had been thought a suicide. A young girl about eighteen years old was found in the river. The apparent cause of death was drowning. The autopsy showed she was two months pregnant, and we found a small caliber bullet hole behind her left ear. It was but a few days after our report that a young man who was seeing this girl was arrested, and consequently convicted of murder....'

"Dr. Swift then pointed to a refrigerated glass case that they use for identification purposes. He explained, 'When we don't know the identity, and the Missing Persons Bureau doesn't either; then we skin the fingertips to obtain *latent prints* to send to the FBI.'

"Next, Dr. Swift pointed to huge drawers, and said, 'The rest of the bodies are stored in these. Last week, you may have heard or read in the papers about the three bodies that burned in a boxcar down in The Hole? These are the three vagrants who have not been identified yet.'

"He bent over, and pulled out one drawer at a time until the three bodies were lying in plain view. He then continued, 'The freezing of a body only stops the decomposition, but not the odor.'

"Boy, as soon as he spoke, the sweet, sickening smell of burnt flesh filled my nostrils."

After Ken said this, Harry asked, "What did you do? Did you pass out?"

Ken followed with….

"No, but I swallowed hard, and leaned over for a closer look. I don't like dead bodies; but there was no skin on them, and so I felt very impersonal to the scene in front of me…. The legs of the first one had its muscles exposed, and it looked like a picture from my high school biology book. As I thought of this, I heard someone behind me wretch. The sound of puke hitting the floor made me jump. I turned to see a blond-haired guy — *white as a sheet*, turn and run from the room, with Sgt. Scharf running after him. I looked back toward the bodies, and was certainly glad to see Dr. Swift bend down, and close the drawers slowly, one by one, until the room was orderly once more.

"Seeking to find Sgt. Scharf, we stepped carefully over the mess on the floor, and went to the door. I glanced back to see Dr. Swift taking a mop from a closet."

"Crappy job, right?" Harry commented.
Vern added, "I can't wait to learn about the morgue. Was that it for the training that day?"

"Hell, no," Ken replied, and continued.

"The rest of the day was pretty slow. We headed back to the classroom, and there were guys going and coming from the morgue all afternoon. Finally, an hour before we got to go home, we all went to the gym for a workout.

"Sgt. Scharf made it fun by being our judo instructor — or at least *he* called it that. He was good — *damn good*, and I marveled at his quickness. He taught us how to put an arm lock on a drunk, or any person we felt needed it.

"I still can remember the pain in my arm as he applied the pressure in demonstration. The Sarge was very thorough, and would go over it again and again until we learned automatically the particular hold that he was teaching. Each hold had a purpose for a certain type of self-protection, and for controlling any individual, regardless of size.

"I was really impressed with the baton, commonly called a night stick or club. It seems as though the baton would carry its discipline very well in a free-for-all. However, I soon learned it had many other uses. We were taught to jab with it in the right places; how to release it when someone had a grip on the other end; and also, to fight with it efficiently in close quarters.

"Using three or four policemen, we were taught to make a human ladder with the baton, which could be used to reach a window, a high fence, or a low roof. In fact, the damn club was a *tool* more than a weapon; and never were we talked into or encouraged to hit anyone on the head with it. That was more or less left unsaid, and to our own judgment."

I interrupted Ken's storytelling by entering the room with a full platter. I put it on the coffee table, and said, "O.K. you guys.... If you're going to sit another two hours yacking, then you better have a sandwich. Here's some egg salad sandwiches and cookies...and a couple of beers to wash it down. You have to have your strength when you get to that class in the gym."

The guys smiled, and Ken continued.

"One of the guys had some previous experience in judo and wrestling, and he just *had* to show it. The Sarge was demonstrating how to break a hold that some criminal might get you in, and he was uncanny—quick as a cat. After demonstrating how to break each hold, he had us try it out on each other. I was glad when my buddy Beeper, former co-worker at A.O. Smith, came over to work with me.

"Meanwhile, *Old Smart Ass* literally challenged the Sarge to break a hold he put on him. We all stopped to watch the show, and you could tell by the men's faces that some were for Old Smart Ass, and others were for the Sergeant. I personally hoped the Sarge would teach him a lesson.

"The big guy came up from behind the Sarge, reached under both armpits, and put a Full Nelson on him, saying, 'Get out of this one, Sarge!'

"The Sergeant slowly said to us, 'Move in a circle.' He wanted us all to see.

"We made the circle—looking like slow-motion dancers, and the Sergeant said evenly 'To break this hold, put your left foot back behind you, and behind the assailant's left leg, and lock it. Then, throw your body backwards to make him fall on his back with you entirely on top of him. The weight of your body hitting the street with the assailant under you will break the hold.... Any questions?'

"No one answered, as it was quite clear what to do.

"The Sergeant said, 'Okay, release.'

"But big Old Smart Ass just applied more pressure. You could see the necks swell, and turn red on both men; and we all realized he had no intention of letting go. They stood locked for several seconds, and suddenly the Sergeant's *right* foot streaked back behind him, and behind Old Smart Ass; and in one motion they both were falling backwards to the mat. Smart Ass's body smacked the canvas with the Sarge on top, and a big whoosh of air added to the crescendo of a groan that came from Smart Ass's mouth. He rolled over onto his stomach, and his arms spread-eagled.

"Sgt. Scharf bounced up on his feet. He glanced around, and said, 'I guess I should have told you, either foot will work.'

"The body on the mat was gasping for air with the wind knocked out of him. The Sergeant said 'That's all. Hit the showers!'

He turned, and walked from the gym.

"Several guys went on the mat, and pounded Old Smart Ass's back, while others helped him to his feet."

Ken stood up, and said, "Well, guys, that's about it for today. I don't want to spoil it for you by telling you everything."

As Harold and Vern stood up, they said, "Thanks, Ken," and headed to the door.

At the doorway, Vern said, "We'll let you know how we do in class."

Harold added, "or if we pass out in the morgue."

Everyone laughed.

CHAPTER NINETEEN

Several months later, on December 9th, 1958, the children and I were invited to accompany Ken as distinguished guests at the Milwaukee Civic Heroism Award Dinner. Chief of Police, Howard O. Johnson, presented Ken with the Civic Heroism Award (plaque), an official commendation which, in part, read:

> *"performing a deed of outstanding service with exceptional devotion to duty, loyalty to his oath of office, and to his obligations as a law enforcement officer in a praiseworthy and admirable manner exemplifying to a high degree the traditions of the Milwaukee Police Department."*

The Chief ordered that this *citation*—or *commendation* as we call it today, would become a permanent part of Ken's departmental personnel file. Along with this, Ken was awarded a choice of vacations to take when he returned to active police duty.

When Ken returned to our table, Mickey shouted, "Daddy, did we win?"

Chief Howard O. Johnson, far left, presented Ken (2nd from left) with the Civic Heroism Award

Chief Howard O. Johnson was a 23-year veteran of the Milwaukee Police Department when promoted to the rank of Chief of Police in 1957. Three years later, the Department had grown to 1,869 members. During Chief Johnson's term (1957-1964), the Underwater Investigation Unit was established along with the Harbor Patrol. He modernized the Department's tabulating system, making possible the procurement of criminal records in just minutes. He established the "roving" patrol wagon, and developed a standardized traffic accident form, which was instituted statewide. Chief Johnson, as a member of the State Street Advancement Association, is responsible for the practice of recognizing police officers and exemplary citizens, "who assisted the Department in some significant manner." He would annually present them with the Civic Heroism Award. *(www.city.milwaukee.gov)*

The civic heroism award winner and the runnersup were honored Tuesday night at a dinner at the Miller Inn, 3931 W. State st. From left are (lower) Patrolmen Stephen Kwasniewski of 7912 W. Burdick av.; Kenneth Stanelle of 5569 N. 54th st., the winner; William Kasten of 3625 N. 82nd st.; (upper) Robert Weigman of 3166 S. 80th st.; Robert B. Kliesmet of 1755 N. Pulaski st., and Harold Gillman of 5450 N. 55th st. Stanelle helped save the life of his partner, Kasten, in a street fight.

—Journal Staff

Kenneth Stanelle Given City Hero Award At Dinner

NORTHWEST REPORT

Patrolman Kenneth G. Stanelle of 5569 N. 54th St., was awarded the third annual civic heroism award of the State Street Advancement association at a dinner last night at the Miller Inn, 3931 W. State St. Also honored was William G. Kasten, 3625 N. 82nd St., who was a runner-up for the award.

Both are policemen in district No. 3, and both were slashed several times with knives in a street fight Nov. 28, 1957. Stanelle, who is credited with saving the life of his partner, Kasten, was selected for the award by a jury of three civic leaders from a list of officers cited for bravery submitted by the police department.

the State Street Advancement association.

Injuries incurred by the two officers necessitated their being off duty for the past year. Kasten returned to duty a week ago Monday, but Stanelle is still at home. Both consider themselves extremely fortunate to be alive, since Stanelle suffered severe facial cuts requiring plastic surgery, and he still suffers dizzy spells caused by a nerve injury. Kasten incurred serious cuts on the leg including severing of a main artery which required grafting operations. He was hospitalized for three months.

chael, 7, Peggy, 2, and David, 3 months. Kasten, 29 has two sons, Billy, 5-1/2, and Scott, 16 months. He has been with the force since January, 1953.

Another Milwaukee-Northwest Patrolman who was guest of honor at the dinner and runner-up for the award is Harold Gillman, 5450 N. 55th St. Three other nominees honored are Robert B. Kliesmet, Stephen L. Kwasniewski and Robert L. Weigman.

Citations Go to Policemen
Two Were Wounded

Two policemen who were severely wounded in fighting off a knife attack received commendations Thursday from Police Chief Howard O. Johnson.

Patrolman Kenneth G. Stanelle, 30, of 5569 N. 54th st., was cited for "unusual courage and reaction in the face of great odds."

Patrolman William G. Kasten, 28, of 3625 N. 82nd st., also was cited.

Not Back to Duty

Neither officer has returned to duty since the fight occurred last Nov. 28 in front of a tavern in the 2900 block of W. Greves st.

Stanelle, who was slashed in the face, was hospitalized until

K. Stanelle   W. Kasten

Jan. 8. He still is undergoing treatment by a plastic surgeon.

Kasten was cut from the abdomen to the knee. He was hospitalized until Feb. 21.

One Man Killed

Stanelle and Kasten were attacked by two men and three women. Stanelle emptied his revolver at one man, killing him.

The commendations also provided choice of vacations for both officers, three extra off-days for Stanelle and one for Kasten.

Interesting Side Note: The Civic Heroism Award Dinner was held on December 9th, 1958. One year earlier, Ken and Bill were in the hospital for a few months. It is stated in the above article that Ken and Shirley's third child, David [David Patrick Stanelle], was 3 months old at the time of the award ceremony. If one puts "two and two together," it is easy to figure out when David was conceived (see Chapter 16).

CHAPTER TWENTY

Ken got a lot of naptime in, and became stronger every day. Shortly after the Civic Heroism Award Dinner, he was admitted to Mount Sinai Hospital. Compared to what he had gone through earlier in the year, it wasn't a scary thing—just much more lonesome. Bill would not be going with him, and even though I would continue being by his side, it was a good thing he would not have to stay long.

The surgeons re-cut his face, so that as he aged, the scars would go with the lines of his skin in a normal way. It didn't happen right away, but eventually, the scars were hardly visible.

Unfortunately, the hidden ones were still there.

****

Recovery time was rest, taking Freddy for walks, getting weekly therapy, and futzing around our new house. Ken also liked to go grocery shopping with me, especially in a larger store. Sometimes, we would forget, and go on the aisle that featured pickles. After opening a jar of pickles back at home, Ken gulped one down, and "Ow!" he groaned with a swipe of his hand to his throat. A hidden injury jumped out at him. His saliva gland had been cut and sewn together, but now it couldn't function. The saliva juices rush to the front when the brain tells it about something tart; but the juices can't go anywhere, and cause extreme pain.

A quick swallow of the pickle helped the pain go away.

****

Sometime during the beginning of 1959, the doctor finally gave his blessings for Ken to return to work. *Sadly*, the Department gave him an office job, because they didn't want to start him with the strain of street work. He wasn't happy, because he was *"stuck behind a desk."*

One day while leaving, Ken stepped into the elevator to go down to the first floor; and right before the door shut, the Chief slipped in. They exchanged *hello's*, and before they hit first floor, Ken got a *spell,* and passed out. The ambulance was called, and they rushed him to the hospital.

This time, a neurosurgeon was called in; and after days of examinations, it was determined that the *concussion* was the culprit. The doctor told us, "Normally, the skull has room for the brain to swell. A lot of things can make the brain swell; for instance, stress or pain.... In Ken's case, his skull was damaged, and there isn't room for his brain to swell. When this happens, he passes out."

The Chief had no choice but to issue Ken a *Disability Retirement.*

WHAT A BLOW!

The reason behind this was strictly policy: A policeman on the Milwaukee Department always wore his gun. The exception was the shower or when he went to bed, which at that time, he shoved it under his bed pillow. In Ken's case, a slight bump on the head, and he could be out—leaving him open to someone stealing his gun.

When Ken told me this, my mind flooded with memories of Ken and his *pride* in carrying his gun. His pride in *protecting others.*

Before the injury, he used to sit on the front porch with Freddy by his side, and he'd watch Mickey play on the sidewalk. His gun was in its holster. He explained how one officer got busted, because he was sitting in his yard, and there was trouble a couple of houses away. The officer ran to help, but didn't have his gun on. He was put on a two-week suspension.

One time I remember, we hired a babysitter, and planned to go to a movie. We hadn't gone far from the house when Ken remembered he was out of cigarettes. We pulled up by a nearby drugstore, and Ken went in. I waited in the car…and *waited and waited;* and began to suspect something had gone wrong.

Ken had walked in on a robbery! I kept watching the door; and finally the door opened, and I saw Ken with his gun out, and his prisoner handcuffed. Ken pushed his prisoner in front of him as they walked to a nearby call box. The police wagon came, and took charge of the prisoner.

We missed the movie; but that was part of being a policeman—*and* a policeman's wife. An ice cream soda in the drug store was the next best option. After that, Ken took me home, and went to the station to fill out a report.

Due to the enforced Disability Retirement, those days were now behind us.

PART TWO:

Second Journey

As told by Kenneth Stanelle's wife, Shirley Elaine Stanelle

CHAPTER ONE

How does one feel about losing a job you really loved? Ken had pulled me along in that journey for *seven years* by telling me about things that went on—*even though they were all told in class not to tell their wives.* I guess if the wives belong to a gym or coffee klatch meeting, they could gossip about the goings on; but Ken and I had always been a team. I think if more wives knew what went on, they wouldn't be leaving their husbands or filing for a divorce so quickly.

While Ken and I adjusted to our new life, I could not stop thinking about Ken's life as a police officer—how life became so very different in such a short time. I will never forget the stories....

One of the times when we were living in an upstairs apartment, with steps going down the back, Mickey and I had some excitement. I was at the stove preparing supper when we heard footsteps bounding up the stairs, followed by heavy boots. The back door to our apartment flew open, and a young lady came running in, and right after her was her motorcycle ex-boyfriend. They ran through the living room, and out the front door. I immediately called the police station. Ken heard in his squad car, and was there in minutes. He found the guy running; and chased him through the neighborhood, jumping over fences, and almost losing it on toys in a back yard. His partner drove around the block, and stopped the guy. The young woman got back in her own apartment downstairs from us. We knew she was fearful of this former boyfriend. Ken had spoken with her numerous times.

****

One story made me feel good. It showed me that Ken was a *father* as well as a policeman. No father wants a kid written up just because he goofed. A good scolding might do the trick….

Ken strolled down a sidewalk one evening, while serving the area as a beat cop. He was heading toward Mr. Cooper's little grocery store, which still had fruit outside in wooden bins and trays. As Ken approached Mr. Cooper's store, two young boys, about thirteen, came out of the store. Not seeing Ken, each grabbed a couple pieces of fruit, and headed down the block laughing. Ken quickened his step, and quickly caught up to them. He was able to grab one of the boys by the scruff of the neck, as the other boy ran down the alley. Ken pulled him into the alley beside the store, and shoved his catch against the wall.

"Okay, kid, what's your name?" he thundered at the boy.
"Eddie"
"Eddie who?"
"Eddie Kowalski."
"What are you doing, stealing Mr. Cooper's apples?"
"I didn't."
"Don't lie to me. I saw you. Empty your pockets."
The boy looked scared, and did as he was told.
"Okay, Eddie, we're marching right back to Mr. Cooper's. You're returning the apples, and apologizing…. Or would you *rather* go to the police station with me?"
"No, sir."

"And you can tell your friend that the next time I catch either of you loitering around here, I'll take you in. Got it?"

"Yes, sir," Eddie replied with great relief.

When I heard that story, I hoped that young Eddie would always remember it.

****

Then there was the time Ken went to work, and was copying the chalked descriptions that were listed:

> Steven Rawson, 3342 N. 16th Street, Age 6
> Ht 3'5", 65lbs., brown eyes, red hair, freckles, wearing blue jeans and tee-shirt
> Missing since 8:00 a.m. July 12th, 1956

We knew the Rawson family for five years, and especially little "Steve" as we called him. The Rawsons lived next door to Ken's cousin, and his folks were invited to the poker games and other parties that we attended....

"Something must really be troubling to make him do a thing like this," Ken thought.

Checking Steve's usual haunts was the first thing on his list. Ken walked unusually fast to cover them. Berry's sand-lot game was in the late innings; and he talked to several of Steve's friends, but no one had seen or heard from him. In fact, they needed another player, and thought he would come for sure.

Ken turned east toward the river, and checked the old pier where the water was only a few feet deep. Occasionally the kids took a dip there—they weren't supposed to, but they did anyway.

It was getting late, and Ken had covered every known spot. He was getting hungry, and headed to the little café near the school. When he walked through the door, he immediately saw Steve sitting there complete with his backpack. He ambled in, and climbed on the empty stool next to him.

"Hiya, Steve."

"Hi, Mr. Stanelle."

"Where have you been?"

"Walking."

"Walking," Ken repeated. "Where to?"

"I'm running away forever and ever," he replied.

"That's an awfully long time," Ken said. "Mind telling me why?"

"Oh, it's nothing," he mumbled.

"Well, it's got to be something to make you do this, Steve. How 'bout it?"

"Well......," he stammered, "it's that new baby sister of mine. We just got her from the hospital last week, and everybody is gushing all over the house because of how cute she looks. They never once pay any attention to me anymore. So, I'm running away forever and ever, and never come back," he said firmly.

"I might be just like you, Steve," Ken countered. "There are times that I would like to run away, myself, but can't."

"Why?" he asked. "You're all growed up."

"Because I know that my family needs me, and that things just couldn't be the same with me gone. Just like you, Steve," he continued. "Your mother needs you, now more than ever."

"Why?" he asked.

"Well," Ken explained, "who's going to go run to the refrigerator, and get the baby's bottle, so your mother can feed her; or help her set the table, or play with your sister to keep her from crying? Your mother is depending on you for help, and you just can't let her down at a time like this."

"Gee, I never thought of it this way," little Steve said. He sat in silence for a moment and then asked, "Do you really think she needs my help?"

"Definitely," Ken affirmed.

"Then I suppose I had better go home," he said.

"Before you do that Steve, how about joining me in a dish of ice cream?"

"Okay," Steve said, and you could see his eyes light up.

"You order," Ken told him, "and I'll make a phone call to tell your mother how I'm going to spoil her son's supper.... Then maybe *she'll* be able to eat *hers*."

****

The stories were many, and I was always interested—especially when Ken went *undercover*, and could be someone else. There was the time that the *push* was on the bookies that holed up in the various taverns, and also on the under-aged drinkers....

It was 9:30 p.m. when Ken, *dressed in plain-clothes,* entered the San Francisco Bar on Wells Street. While Ken ordered a drink, a patrolman entered; and after looking around, he went out again.

The owner confided to Ken, "Those guys are checking for minors—the *heat* is really on. Why Saturday night, this place was crawling with them. I don't know how dumb they think we are, but *I* can spot those bastards *every time*.

Ken left at midnight, and returned at 1:00 a.m. He told the bartender he had gone out to eat. There didn't appear to be any minors, and all of the patrons appeared to be about 30 years or older...but there was a girl called Sylvia, and she promised the bartender a good night kiss. She kept asking Ken where he worked, and told him to be there Saturday night; and he could expect a passionate kiss just like she gave the bartender.

Ken's identity had gone undetected, which made him proud.

****

Ken and Bill Dressed as Undercover Cops

Ken got such a kick out of telling about the training for *prostitute hunting*. One officer at his precinct was short, slim, and good-looking; and once in a while, he got the job of being dressed like a prostitute—high heels, black mesh nylons, a short skirt that would swing when he sauntered, and of course, a black blouse with a low-cut neckline and false boobs.

He would walk on the sidewalk on certain downtown streets in hopes to attract a client. Ken's job was to tail him in an unmarked car a good distance away, or park the car nearby until a *john* would come along, and they could arrest him. Sometimes the "prostitute" would get in the car, and be whisked away, making it necessary for the police car to follow, and then make the arrest.

****

Another time, Ken was going to have a closer relationship with a real prostitute. He was pretty excited, and I had to help test his collar and upper part of his sports coat. The prostitutes could feel if the pinpoint of the badge had been stuck through the material, so we examined it carefully. When he came home that night, and needed to explain the lipstick on his collar, he quickly started….

"Well…there was this party at the fancy Westlock Hotel, with rumors that there would be lots of prostitutes available. I was assigned for duty, with Steve Ingle following me. I had to get a *jade* to leave with me, and go to the saloon we had under suspicion—which was a *bawdy* house. So, I got to the hotel, parked, and look around. Ingle wasn't parking, or I couldn't see him; so I was thinking, *'What the hell happened to him?'"*

"I entered the fancy lobby, and started to mingle with other business-looking guys, and went to the cash bar for a cocktail. All of a sudden, I feel someone next to me, and a sultry voice says, 'Hi handsome. I don't usually see you around here.'"

"She was a looker, too. Blonde hair, wine-colored dress *with her boobs popping out*, and long, dangling earrings."

"I told her, 'That's because I just got into town, and my association told me to check this place out for some action.' Then I said to her, 'I'm having a martini; can I buy you one, too?'"

"'That would be nice… and where did you fly in from?'"

"'Green Bay; I'm with the Packers.'"

"'Oh, honey, I love football players…. So, you dance? I love to dance,' and she guided me to the dance floor."

"Then she wrapped her hands around my neck and jacket, and she very skillfully checked for the telltale pin marks."

"Meanwhile, I'm trying to glance around without being obvious, and watching for Ingle. *'He better not have left me hanging here by myself,'* I thought."

"Then the jade cooed in my ear, 'Come on, sweetie, let's go where I can hear myself think. It's so noisy in here, and there's a quieter place just down a few blocks.'"

"'I'm all for that,' I answered."

"We got in the car, a BMW Coupe—the force keeps this car on hand for special occasions. I pulled out when I saw Ingle. That made me feel better…until further down the road when I couldn't see him in my rearview. *'He better be following me,'* I said to myself."

"I parked in front of a harmless looking saloon, and we went in; and with her arms around me, she whispered, 'Follow me, and for only $200.00, I will make you *very* happy.'"

"I pulled out my billfold, handed her the bills, and started up the stairs behind her. We entered the room, and she closed the door…only to have it opened, shortly after by Ingle and the rest of the guys, who came in."

"There were 10 busts that night, and the madam was speechless…."

"What was Steve Ingle's story?" I asked Ken. "You said he wasn't behind you before the club."

"Well, he was caught behind a traffic light; and I should have noticed, and pulled over and waited for him. He called in to the captain, who told him where I was headed."

I announced, "Thank heavens, or I might have lost you to a prostitute!" Then I grabbed him, and we hurried off to bed.

I made a mental note to be sure to read that report when he brought it home.

****

It may have looked funny to most people to see their husband go to work in dirty jeans and an old checkered and torn shirt, but Ken's job one week entailed hanging out at a particular tavern at the Starburn Inn. *He told them he just got laid off….*

Ken's job was to hang out, watch television, smoke cigarettes, sip a drink, play pool, and get to be friends with the owners. He didn't go every day, but maybe two or three days in a row. A typical day had Ken spying on a man named Hank. Hank would enter the tavern, and say to the bartender, "Let me see the sheets."

The bartender reached under the bar, and produced a folded newspaper. Hank opened it, and sorted through a stack of blueish-green papers, which were most likely racing forms of some kind.

Hank and the bartender proceeded to talk over the races for the day. They were looking at a copy of *Illinois Sports News*, which sold for 25 cents. They were discussing which horse to bet on. They liked a horse called Blue Note and another one called Twisted Wrist. Hank then proceeded to write down his entry on the sheet. They both bet on a different horse in the same race, and decided to split the winnings. They talked over the racing forms for about a half an hour before Hank said, "Are you going to call Louie?"

The bartender said it wasn't necessary; as if he wanted to see him, he could walk over to Louie's house — evidently it must be close by. He said, "We're going down there tomorrow, anyway; so it doesn't make any difference." He stated that he had to pick up the newsboy downtown and another guy, as they wanted to go along with them.

The bartender paid no attention to Ken. He talked freely, and never gave him a second glance.

One day, as Ken was hanging out, and practicing pool by himself, he was wishful that it might be the day. He thought, *"According to last week, this is the day the bookie should come in."*

The door opened, and in walks one of Ken's cousins — Herb.

"Kenny, what are you doing here? Sneaking out on the old lady?" Herb snickered.

Ken quickly responded, "Herbie, get over here, and see if you can beat me!"

When Herbie got close to him, Ken hissed in his ear, "Get outta here. It's a bust."

Herb quickly announced, "Another time, cousin. I just remembered that my old lady is going to want the car! See ya!"

Luckily, Herb caught on, and left. Ken breathed a sigh of relief.

Ken finally had enough information, and a hit was planned. At the precise time the bookie appeared, Ken, *from inside the tavern,* walked to the front door, and opened it. He flicked out his remaining cigarette, turned around; and his fellow officers rushed in, and arrested Hank and the bartender.

When they realized what was happening, Ken joined in on the arrest; and the bartender shouted, "Not you!"

It was one of Ken's finer moments.

****

So many wonderful memories…*but what were we going to do now?* Since Ken could no longer work as a policeman, his pension was dropped to 75% of his regular wage. We just bought a house…. This prompted me to bring out the pad of paper, and start figuring again:

1. Joe would let Ken work for him painting houses *(but that wasn't enough).*
2. I could keep teaching ceramics in our basement *(but with just getting started, my classes are too small).*
3. I'll have to find a job; and since Ken has to stay home for a while, he will be home to get Mickey to school, and take care of the baby.

It wasn't an ideal situation for either of us, but we would try it.

****

I was lucky to get a job at a high school in the library. I think I typed every card in that library. At least it seemed that way. During my lunch hour, I would take the time to order supplies for my ceramic classes. Meanwhile, Ken busied himself with the ceramics and with the clay. He began designing patterns and tools to be used by hand for creating objects. He also became friends with other studio owners, and they kept encouraging him.

I had shared with Ken my dream of being an art teacher while we were dating, and it never happened; so he believed that ceramics would fill the void. The seed had been planted in Ken, and little did we know that it would someday lead to an entirely different journey.

CHAPTER TWO

Our lives became very different. We worked long hours at our new odd jobs. One day, we got a call from Beeper and Betty, and they hollered into the phone, "The sun is shining! Let's go on a picnic!"

Beeper and Betty had become good friends with us, and it would be a welcome change to quit working in the basement for a while. We agreed to meet them at the lakefront park on Lake Michigan.

That day, I made potato salad, and took pickles; and Betty brought deviled eggs and some hotdogs to grill. Their little son, Pokey, along with Mickey, enjoyed running and playing on the gym equipment. Peggy, Betty, and I sat on a blanket; and the guys brought along cane poles for all of us to fish.

But this day was not like other times. Beeper had trained to become a police officer at the same time as Ken. Beeper continued to talk of his police experiences, while Ken could not.

I couldn't help thinking about how our friendship began, so I said, "Betty, remember the day we first met here for a picnic? It was a beautiful day in July. The guys were in training, and I asked you if Beeper was as crabby by the end of the week as Ken was. Remember how you answered? You spit out, 'Crabby! I'm ready to tell him to get out by Wednesday; and then on weekends he falls all over himself trying to make up for it.'"

That's how Ken was. On Monday, he was cool, and each day he would tighten up a little more until *Friday*, when he was like a bowstring ready to let fly. Then on Saturday, he would wind down, and on Sunday he could finally really relax—and that's when I let him know *in no uncertain terms* that his behavior was *unacceptable*. He then apologized to me and to Mickey.

****

I don't know how much Beeper shared with Betty, but Ken told me about their first day on the pistol range....

Ken had been shooting by the early age of twelve, and was a pretty good shot. But Beeper never had any experience with guns. Ken, a hunter most of his life, was amazed at how many would-be cops never fired a weapon in their lives.

One day after class, Ken approached Beeper, and they talked.

"I hear you're not doing so good with the canon, ol' buddy."

"Hell, Ken," Beeper answered. "I shake so damn bad, it's a wonder I haven't killed the Sergeant."

"Look Beeper," Ken said, "let's talk to Sgt. Patton, and see if we can't shoot extra on Saturday maybe."

"Naw," he said, "Betty would have a fit, and besides...I don't even like the damn gun."

"Look friend, you better learn to like it – no, on second thought, you better learn to love it! From what I hear, it's all you've got in some cases to save your hide."

Beeper looked thoughtfully, and said, "I suppose you're right; but I just can't get the hang of it, and I don't like it."

"Well, you keep Saturday morning open for some shooting; and in the afternoon, let's have a picnic with our families."

Beeper smiled, and said, "What if Sarge won't let us?"

"Then we'll have the picnic anyway, and I'll even talk to the Sarge for ya."

The next day at the range, Ken talked to Sgt. Patton, and explained Beeper's problem.

Ken returned home excitedly, "Shirley, it was just too beautiful for words! Sgt. Patton okayed it for Saturday at 9:30

a.m. He has some detectives qualifying at 8:30, but they should be done in time."

Ken explained how he felt he had made an ass of himself when he innocently asked Sgt. Patton, "Why do the detectives have to qualify? Can't they shoot?"

Sgt. Patton got a grin on his face, and said, "Sure they can shoot, but every cop on this Department must re-qualify with the .38 Police Special every six months for as long as they are on the Department. You didn't think we would let them get rusty, did you?"

That Saturday, Betty and I took her car, and our paraphernalia for a nice picnic. We secured our place at the park. Meanwhile, Ken drove Beeper to the Safety Building, and later he told me what had transpired:

"We went inside, and down the hall to the door marked Pistol Range. We started down the steel steps. We could hear the flat crack of pistols before we opened the door, and we knew the detectives weren't finished.

"We remained silent, and just watched. There were about eight to ten positions, and a man at each position. Each man pushed the button that sent the target running to its position downrange, fifty feet away. The targets were swinging as each man stood quietly, and his target stopped. It was deathly quiet; and then Sergeant Patton gave the signal. Each man slowly raised his revolver, and began firing.

"Beeper jumped a little with each shot. The firing was slow, very slow; and each man raised his weapon, aimed carefully, and fired. Finally the rounds had been expelled, and the targets skittered back to their start positions. Each man removed his target, and walked over to Sgt. Patton's desk.

"One of them yelled, 'Hey Jim, ready to count the scores?'

"'Damn right, I am!'

"'Go to it!' he replied.

"First of all, I knew they were detectives, because I had seen them around the Safety Building. Secondly, I couldn't figure out where they got off calling Sgt. Patton 'Jim.'

"Each target was brought before Sgt. Patton, and the Sergeant would add up the score, and write it on the corner of the target. I raised up on my toes, and then realized what he was doing. He finished, looked up, and said, 'Damon, you got it.... You got the highest score.'

"The other four men whooped or hollered their dismay, and a few slapped Damon on his back. Then each man reached in his pocket, and paid Damon a dollar bill; and they left talking and laughing all the way up the stairs.

"I turned to Beeper, and said in amazement, 'Did you see that?'

"'Yeah,' Beeper answered. 'And they didn't even sign their targets.'

"I noticed Beeper's color wasn't too good, but I said nothing.

"The silence continued until Sgt. Patton got up from his desk, and said 'Hi fellas, how goes it?'

"We both shrugged our answer, and Sgt. Patton walked to the gun closet, and pulled out a .38 Special for Beeper.

"'What about me?' I questioned, 'I want to shoot, too!'

"'You don't need the practice, Stanelle; your shooting is just fine.'

"I normally consider myself to be even-tempered; but I got all fired up, and said, 'Look, Sgt Patton, until I can shoot like those last five Tom, Dick, and Harry's, I'm *not* doing just fine, and dammit I'm going to *shoot* like them!'

"A smile slowly spread over the Sergeant's face; and he turned, and got out another .38 from the cabinet.

"'Alright, Stanelle. If you want to shoot that bad, you can shoot.'

"Meanwhile, the Sergeant told Beeper that he had observed his performance on the pistol range. He explained what his problem was, and told him that if he got a bullseye, it was only by accident.

"Beeper then loaded up, and snapped the cylinder shut. He stepped into the firing booth, and pushed the starter button. The target obeyed, sailing down to the end, and wobbling into place.

"Sgt. stepped in behind him, and told him, 'Go ahead, and fire out the rounds."

"Beeper fired, *Pow, pow, pow!* Then a pause, and *Pow!* Another pause, and *Pow!*

"The Sarge reached in, pushed the return button for the target, and then walked to his desk, and said to Beeper, 'Olson, that's got to be the worst shooting I've seen in a long time. Let's sign you up for the next six Saturdays. Stanelle, you can come along, and help coach him, if you want.'"

When the guys met us at the lakefront park, Beeper hesitated before telling Betty how bad he did, and that the next six Saturdays would be taken. We all agreed that he would be a happier man if he was a better marksman.

CHAPTER THREE

"'Bye honey, I'll see you at five! Oh, I have everything ready for you to put in the crockpot, okay? Don't forget to get Mickey from school! Love you!"

I backed out the Renault, and raced toward the high school. I wasn't nicknamed "Lead-Foot" for nothing.

Ken still struggled with the great changes we faced. It was hard to fathom that his days as a policeman were over. He didn't care if he had to work nights or days or uniform or plainclothes.... *"Just let me be a cop!"*

He knew he had to snap out of it, because I was counting on him. Luckily, it was summer; and he headed for the garage—Peggy in one arm, and the playpen in the other. A few weeks earlier, he had decided to sacrifice the car space in the garage to a *Ken* space. A space to think or experiment with clay, or practice building up his muscles and nerves in his hand.

There was clay in the studio, so he sat down, and started forming it into something.... *But what?*
There has got to be a way to make a three-dimensional vessel. *But how does one do this?* Then he remembered both his mother and sister cutting out material from a pattern. The more he thought about it, the more elated he got. But there wasn't room on the table. The table was all set for class that evening.

He started to draw a few simple shapes on a sketch pad; and when he was satisfied, he cut those shapes out of newspaper. Carefully picking his patterns up, and he made room for rolling out the clay. He had been practicing rolling the clay with a simple rolling pin, and was able to roll it perfectly to one quarter-inch thickness without guide sticks. The bakery days of rolling out dough came in handy.

Ken was just figuring this out to perfection, when the baby whimpered. With a wee bit of exasperation, he said, "What's the matter, honey? Are you hungry, wet, or what?? We'll go inside, and see if we can help you out."

So he picked her up, and with Freddy tailing them, headed inside. He changed Peggy's diaper, fed her, shuckled her to sleep; and then hurried back to the garage, where he quickly placed the patterns on the the rolled-out clay, and then cut out the clay pieces. He had to hurry and finish one piece before Peggy woke. Just one for now, and maybe one additional piece after he picked up *Mick* (as we called our firstborn during these years).

Ken had some dried scrapings from cleaning greenware, and he mixed it with a little water, making a paste. The clay he rolled out wasn't stiff enough to work with, so he thought he could check on the baby. While in the house, he put supper in the crockpot, and off he hurried back out again.

He scored the edges of a flat, triangle shape with a tool. Then he applied the paste to three pieces, and stood them up one by one. This made a small, triangle vase.

"Yes!" he exclaimed to himself. *"When it's set more, and a little drier, I'll clean it up."*

He ran in the house. Peggy was awake, and he said, "Come on sweetie, we have to get Mick." And off he hurried down the sidewalk to the school, which was only a few blocks away.

On the walk home, Ken told Mick about his new discovery. He then said, "Hey Mick, I'll let you play with clay and watch the baby at the same time," adding, "just long enough to give Daddy time to finish his new creation, and surprise Mommy when she gets home."

When I got home later, Ken—with baby in arms, and Mick jumping, was jovial in spirit.

"Quick, come to the garage!" both Ken and Mick called.

I followed them, and a three-foot trophy couldn't have been more important. The vase, though small, was perfect. It looked like it came from a mold. I was amazed and impressed.

Then, of course, the words came tumbling out of Ken's mouth, a mile a minute—elaborating on all his ideas for other designs.

What good medicine that clay was.

CHAPTER FOUR

I became a member of the local ceramic association, and at a meeting shared some of Ken's successes. I suggested they stop in to visit with him. They did; and it was great, because he had someone to talk to during the day to discuss similar subjects. They were all ceramists, and didn't work with raw clay. Instead, they fired slip in a kiln.

As he grew more familiar with the workings of a kiln, he eventually became the go-to repairperson if something went wrong or they needed a new element. Everyone was amazed at his new progress.

One night, when I came home, he showed me around ten new pieces—a swan planter, a Chinese style vase, and many more. Then he asked for a favor. "Honey, can you round up about six or eight kids?"

I was right in the middle of making stir-fry with chicken and vegetables; and so without looking up, or stopping my stirring, I said, "For?"

"I'd like to see if my patterns are easy enough for them to put together."

"Okay, I'm sure my ceramic students have children, and then there are the children next door. When do you want them?"

"Next Saturday."

"Your wishes are my command!"

Ken smiled, and said, "If this pans out like I hope it will, maybe we could write the directions, then type them, and get them run off at your work."

Eight happy kids and a few grownups came on the following Saturday, and everyone had a great time. I made a large pitcher of lemonade for them, and had paper cups handy. Their pieces were not perfect like Ken's, but they understood the directions.

Clay designs using Ken's patterns

Now what shall we do with this newfound information?

Ken already knew. His adult ceramic friends started telling him about the ceramic shows around the country, and there just happened to be one in Detroit, Michigan next month. A friend gave me the telephone number, and I called to see if they had any room. *They did!* I gave them Ken's name, and they would let him pay his booth fee when he arrived.

I found someone who had a mimeograph machine that I could borrow, bought four reams of paper, and Ken started crankin'. *How much for each pattern?* We finally decided to charge fifty cents to three dollars for each, depending on how many sheets of paper each design took. In a few days, he would have to leave; so we carefully packed his samples and patterns in a hard shell suitcase, along with material to put on the table, some clay, tools, and a rolling pin. On Thursday night, I took him to the airport, kissed him goodbye, and wished him good luck.

It was a three-day show, and he had just enough money for a three-nights stay; so that meant he would fly back home when the show was over on Sunday evening.

Sunday night was finally here, and when he got off the plane, he had a big grin on his face. He had two patterns left. That was all.... He almost *sold out!*

Of course, his demonstrations did it. He could talk and work at the same time, and he made it look so easy. Magically another finished piece would appear—e*asy-peasy.*

I had my own activity to share with him, and I could hardly wait to get on the road, and tell him. We weren't even out of the airport, and I had to stop him talking.... "Ken, honey, at the last BSA meeting, Sam told a joke, and I have been repeating it all week so I would remember it. You know, *you* are the story or joke person, and I can *never* remember any—especially the punch line. So here goes: Did you know that when a woman wears a leather dress, a man's heart beats quicker, his throat gets dry, he gets weak in the knees, and he begins to think irrationally? Ever wonder why? It's because she smells like...."

And just before I told the punch line, that darn husband of mine said, "like a new golf bag!"

I couldn't believe it. I finally practiced, and remembered; and he had heard it at the show. I was so deflated; I punched him on the shoulder.

"But, Shirl, give yourself a pat on the back for a job well done. At least you tried," and he laughingly added, *"I could have butted in sooner...."*

****

Our ceramics friends were elated for him, and now they told us about the *BIG* show in New Jersey. It was a four-day event each May, and people went to it from all over the country. It would take some planning and money to get there, and we had six months to plan. Ken got busy creating new designs, and we both had something to look forward to.

Six months later, we were packed, and ready to go to the East coast. We met Ken's folks in Appleton, *ninety miles north of Milwaukee,* and they took the children. Now that the children were taken care of, we arranged with a neighbor to let Freddy out each day, and feed him. It was the tail end of Spring Break, and I wouldn't need to miss work. It was finally time to load the 1951 used Nash station-wagon, say a prayer, and take off to lands we had never been to before.

We headed toward Chicago, and then continued east on I-80. When we got to Pennsylvania, we were thrilled to be on the Turnpike. We never paid to drive on a highway before. But it was nice, and we were able to really move on it. At one of the stops for gas, I was reading that when the Turnpike was built, they tried to lay the route on the southern exposures to let the sun heat the ice and snow on the roads.

We took turns driving and sleeping in the car. It would take us almost two days to get there by Wednesday, set up that day, and be ready for the show Thursday through Sunday. We had enough money along to pay for four nights lodging, the gas, and some food. We sent the booth fee several months before; and we hoped and prayed that the car would take us there and back.

We had our doubts when we got stymied in the outskirts of New Jersey with a circle. *What way were we supposed to go?* Other cars were just zipping along round and round; another spun off to the side road. *Holy Mackerel!* We couldn't pull off anywhere; and luckily locals could see we were from another state, and didn't mow us down. *We made it!*

We left Wisconsin with snow still along the curbs, and were thrilled to see the New Jersey trees in bloom. It was an early window-peeking to springtime. The area of the state that we passed through looked so spacious and farm-like and pretty. In the town itself, there were blossoms everywhere—along the sidewalks, on trees, in the front and back yards of the homes, and in flower baskets hanging in front of stores. The scent of the cherry tree blossoms was almost hypnotizing. We both took a deep breath, and together said *"Aaaaah!"*

The show was held in a large convention center in Asbury Park, New Jersey, where half of the large building butted out over the ocean. I was amazed and delighted to look at the ocean. Ken, of course, had crossed an ocean when he was in the Service; but this was my first experience. Every chance I got during the next four days, I wandered to the back railing to look out at it. To the south, I could see the Boardwalk and vendors set up to sell fresh sea taffy, and a bar advertising itself as the longest bar in the world.

Our booth was upstairs, and it was a busy, bustling place. The upstairs was like a balcony, and we could look down and see the other booths already set up. Music— *"Raindrops Keep Falling On My Head"* softly played over the P.A. system.

Ken had designed and finished over fifty sample pieces. He had printed a stack of patterns, and had extra in a box. On our first day, we were really busy, and people were watching Ken demonstrate his skills. We were delighted that we sold enough patterns for another night's stay. It seemed like everyone wanted to buy the *molds*— which we didn't have, of course.

Ken became friends with Fred, two booths away. Fred asked, "Is that all you're selling…*just patterns?*"

He was a mold-maker, and came from a family of mold-makers in Germany. Besides molds, he also sold a cord with a metal hook on the end called a *mold tie.* It held multiple pieces of the molds together. He said, *"Here,* take half of my supply of ties, and pay me half of what you sell them for." Besides that, he ended up giving Ken a lesson on how to make a mold.

Later, a magazine publisher from California stopped by our booth. After watching Ken demonstrate, he asked him to be a contributor to his magazine, *Popular Ceramics.* Ken liked to write stories, and was pleased at the opportunity to become more deeply involved with the ceramic industry. This was good for his self-respect, and would help erase some of the hurt he still held from being put on Duty Disability.

The show ended, and we were pleased that we were able to pay all our expenses, and still had a little left over. Besides that, friendships, lessons on mold-making, and becoming a magazine writer were enough to give us plenty to discuss on the way home.

Before we knew it, we got home, and Ken left to pick up the children. Poor Mom and Dad! After they had picked up the children, they didn't get all the way back home when Mick started showing red spots. Upon examination, he had chickenpox, and Peggy got it the next day.

CHAPTER FIVE

Ken had been writing for *Popular Ceramics* magazine, and one article he wrote featured a swan-shaped box. He gave the instructions for how to make it, and a finished swan box was pictured. Because of his articles, he started getting calls to teach his techniques at studios around the country, and even as far northeast as New Brunswick, Canada! I would set up his agenda—usually it included a show, and then three or four studios in the same area.

It wasn't ideal for him to be gone one to two weeks, but he was getting very popular; and it made our sales at the shows that much better.

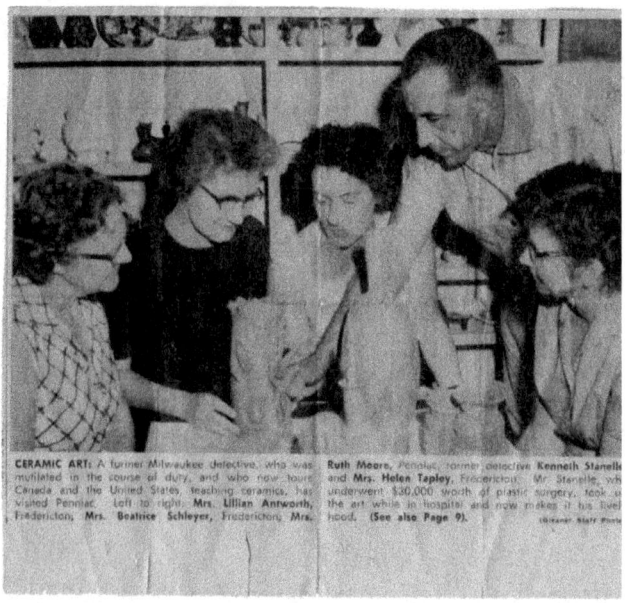

Ken teaching in Penniac, New Brunswick, Canada

Women Onlookers

Ken demonstrating a Drape Mold pot

popular CERAMICS

March, 1962
50c

TRADE MARK REGISTERED — A FRED DE LIDEN PUBLICATION

KEN STANELLE: *Strength through clay* (See page 60)

The Original Ceramic Hobby Magazine—Published for the Hobbyist

KEN STANELLE: Strength Through Clay

By MEL FISKE

INSTINCTIVELY Patrolman Ken Stanelle reached for his gun and started shooting at the two shadowy figures whose knives were slashing him. He fell to the ground in the darkness, still shooting. Then all was quiet again on that dark Thanksgiving night, in 1957.

"In the space of 30 seconds, one man was dead, one wounded, one unconscious with a severe leg wound, and myself with my throat and face cut," Stanelle related. "I stayed conscious long enough to keep control of the situation until help arrived."

The 30 seconds climaxed a "routine" investigation conducted by Stanelle and his partner, both members of the Milwaukee Police Department.

"For three days," Stanelle continued, "my partner and I hung between life and death. It took 370 stitches to put my face back together. After two months, I was released from the hospital. My strength was gone and I had very little muscle control."

At home with his wife, Shirley, and three children, Ken was helped on his slow road to recovery by his family—and his clay. He had found relaxation in ceramics during his seven years on the police force. "I was determined not to be pitied," he said, "and I went into the basement studio and worked with clay. It was work just to wedge it, but ever so slowly my strength and my mind kept improving. With Shirley's constant encouragement, I kept on."

Then back to the hospital he went to undergo months of plastic surgery. Medical science wrought another of its "wonders" and his face was restored almost as it had been before the attack. "When the bandages were removed, some of my ill health went with them," he confessed.

A grateful city presented him with a bronze plaque and the Civic Heroism award in 1958, and, when it was determined that he would never be able to reassume his duties, the city placed him on disability retirement. "This was very hard to take," he said, "but again, I went back to the only thing I could do—ceramics."

While Shirley took a job to help support the family, Ken tended the children and worked hard developing clay slab patterns and his ceramic skills. He took the big plunge two years ago and introduced his drape molds at the Chicago show. He also began teaching and found that his molds and ability as a teacher were immediately recognized and accepted by hobbyists.

Shirley quit her job and joined Ken in a combined effort to make a living at ceramics. They reasoned that since they both loved ceramics and since they both had found strength and tranquility through ceramics, they could not lose, even if they failed in business.

But fail they did not. They set up a greenware warehouse and a ceramic studio. Ken bought an old truck and, instead of waiting for studios and hobbyists to come to S-K Potteries for their supplies, went to them. He covers the entire state of Wisconsin and upper Michigan with his truckful of supplies, including greenware.

"Our business is growing with us," Ken relates happily, "I am still up to my neck in clay and love every minute of it."

Ken offers himself as living proof of the beneficial worth of ceramics in physical therapy. He'll appear before any group of handicapped to show them how ceramics made him whole in body and spirit. But he concentrates his teaching in kindergartens, high schools and hobbyist shows. For he believes that ceramics offers strength to everyone.

It wasn't ideal for me, either! The days weren't so bad, because I was extremely busy; but I would really miss him at night when it was time to go to bed.

One night he called me from a gas station near Chicago. He had been gone two weeks, and he wanted me to know he would be home in two hours and ten minutes.

"Shirl, all I want is to see you naked with a rose in your mouth!"

Like I said, I was lonesome for him, too. Enough to spark the devilishness in me! I thought, *"I'll surprise you, lover,"* as I headed for the basement to search in a few boxes. I found what I was looking for! At Christmas-time, Ken received a dozen plastic, pink roses from the magazine as a thank you. I had just recently packed them away.

About twenty minutes before he would arrive, I got undressed, and put on my robe (*naked underneath, you understand*). I pulled one rose out of the bunch, and sat on the couch. The living room faced the street, and without a foyer, the front door opened directly into it. There was a curtain on the front big-window; but when he drove in the driveway, the lights shown through the curtain. I heard the doorknob turn, threw off the robe, and lay there with a rose in my mouth.

I'm surprised the neighbors didn't come running, or the children wake, because the hootin' and hollerin' and lovin' was mighty wonderful!

****

The next morning, Ken told me about his surprise— one that he would have given me when he got home, *if I hadn't changed the scenery....*

As he left a studio in Canada, Ken asked the studio owner for the directions to a really fine ladies-shop. He wanted to get me a present. She gave him the name of a store and directions, and he found it without any problem. He went in very proud, because he had cash. The very uppity lady looked at him with his jeans, flannel shirt, and big hands with dried clay; and she turned the other way, ignoring him.

Ken waited and waited, and finally *another* snooty lady approached him; and as she looked him up and down said, "You must be in the wrong store."

Ken was shocked and disappointed; and went back to the Canadian studio, *where someone appreciated him*. This time, the studio owner, Elizabeth (*who was not in jeans*), took off her apron, and said, "Let's go."

The ladies-shop owner was surprised to see Ken enter her shop again. But when she saw that he was with Elizabeth, an important customer of hers, she didn't know what to think.

Ken ended up buying me a dress, a matching jacket with mink collar, earrings, and a bracelet to match. He paid *CASH*. They didn't know what to think, because *nobody* has cash, and they apologized over and over again.

Throughout life, and while I waited on customers, that experience would come to mind many times. The outside packaging is not necessarily what is in the inside. And this was only some of the little things he went through for me....

I am happy he was my husband.

CHAPTER SIX

With our small profits, I found a babysitter two times a week, for a few hours, giving Ken some freedom to explore new ideas.... His big hands worked the clay into an oval shape, and then he cut it until he had the answer. He placed the flat side down on a piece of discontinued countertop, and built a box around it with thick slabs of clay.

His friend, Fred, the mold-maker from the New Jersey show, had given him a small jar of mold soap to experiment with; and he brushed that over his oval shape. Now he was ready to pour the plaster into the crude box, and over the clay oval. The finished product would be a plaster box with an oval-shaped cavity. Finally, he could pull off the crudely made clay walls, turn it over with the oval cavity facing up, soap it, and carefully pour plaster into the cavity. *This was Ken's first mold!*

When the solid, plaster oval was dry—in about thirty minutes, he turned his mold over, and released his new solid oval. He then rolled out a large piece of clay, and draped the rolled-out clay over the solid oval. He waited for the draped clay to dry, and then pulled it away. This created the same oval shape, but it was now a hollow oval. He discovered an entirely new type of mold. We called it a *Drape Mold*. A new product was born.

An hour later, he had two hollow clay halves, stiff enough to assemble. He scored them, added a gooey clay mixture, and carefully attached them together. He cut off the top, and flared the edges back to display a handsome vase.

Ken looked around his little shop, and was pleased with himself. But he was shocked to see what a mess he had made. *"Better hurry, and get this mess cleaned up before Shirley gets home from her job at the library,"* he told himself.

There was clay on the floor, and plaster spatters everywhere; and he was a mess—even with some swipes of plaster in his hair!

When he heard the car come in the driveway, and stepped out, he thought, *"Shirley looks grumpier than usual."*

"What's the matter, kiddo?" Ken called.

"Oh, it's that *Mister* Brentmeister again! He wants to make me feel grumpy....*and short*. When he gives me instructions for the day, he delights in standing as tall as he can (he stood six foot three). Ugh! You know, honey, you never make me feel short, even though I'm only five feet tall...and that's only one of the reasons I love you.... *And what happened to you? You look a mess!"*

"Sorry, honey," Ken said. Then he announced, "Come in the garage, and tell me what you think."

We went in the garage, and I saw immediately his new little prize.

"Ken, that's great! Tell me all about what you did here."

As he told me, I was excited for him, and forgot all about Mr. Brentmeister.

Suddenly, we heard the screen door slam, and Mick, racing to us, shouted, "Mom, you're home! It's a good thing, because Peggy just threw up, and Julie [the sitter] is trying to clean it up."

Peggy was one and a half years old with a round face and brown hair. Her eyes lit up whenever her daddy picked her up; and she was cuter than a bug's ear when I dressed her up in a fluffy dress.

"Peggy's making such a mess, Mom. You should see the highchair!"

That evening, we talked about Ken's new experiment. The questions now were *"How could he produce twenty or more to possibly sell at a show?"* *"What could we call it?"* and *"Is this something we could market?"*

The next day at the library during my lunch hour, I looked up books that featured ceramics. It seemed that professors of art classes used various forms, similar to clay draping, and they called it *hump molds* or *slump molds*. Meanwhile, Ken called Fred, (our German mold-maker friend); and he refreshed his memory about Ultracal, the hard finish plaster that mold-makers used to produce their masters. Also, Ken heard that there was a sculptor in Milwaukee who made a few molds, and he visited him the next day to see if he had extra Ultracal plaster to purchase from him.

The next few weeks, I had to coax Ken to see him. He was in the garage making samples and new shapes for molds. He also poured the few molds I had, so the students would have greenware to work on. It didn't take long until a section of the garage had shelves for the molds and a table to do the casting.

Ken making a rooster basket with a Drape Mold

And then one Saturday—*luckily while I was home,* Ken had one of his spells. I quickly called for an ambulance, and also called a friend, who came and sat with the children as I took off after the ambulance.

Sometimes those spells knocked him out or put him in a coma. They carried Ken into the hospital on a gurney, and I parked and hurried in. The lady at the desk told me how to find him. They gave him some kind of shot that brought him to again. I was relieved.

That was the first one since being in our new home. We never knew exactly what brought it on, but he had suffered with pain from an abscess tooth—or it could have been the stress and excitement of creating his new creations.

They kept Ken in the hospital that night. The next day, we talked about it, and I suggested he slow down.

"No way! The harder I work, the less I think about not being in that squad car."

CHAPTER SEVEN

On the two days a week we had our sitter, Ken would load up our little Rambler wagon, which had a rack inserted to hold the greenware that he poured. Off he would go for the northernmost part of the state, where most people didn't even know what the word *ceramic* meant. This was good, because it got him out of the house to meet interesting people, and have more stories to tell.

Ken decided to form some sort of delivery service for the studios in rural areas. *After all, the backbone of the ceramic industry was the basement—or garage, studio,* he thought. Everyone told him it couldn't be done. He knocked on doors, and explained his plan of "Free Delivery Service, Once a Month." Some were skeptical; but after two months, he had a grand total of three confirmed stops.

However, there weren't enough sales to pay for the gas. He would have to have more sales, and that meant getting a bigger vehicle. So, he went looking, and found an old van of ancient vintage. He made shelves in the back with an aisle in between. The shelves had ledges to prevent the greenware from sliding off. A good thick layer of shredded paper was placed on the shelf for greenware. The customer could step up on a stool Ken brought along, walk inside, and select the cast piece he liked. Ken replenished the shelves after each trip. Glazes, clay, molds, and casting slip sat in a pile on the floor under the shelves.

Business increased, and black ink for the *profit-and-loss ledger* was almost in sight when the van broke down beyond repair. The delivery service was suspended until he found a lighter and faster unit—our new *Cerami-van!* Ken was back in business again.

Finally the route covered an 800-mile round-trip, made in three days. The trip didn't cost much, as meals and a bed were free at whatever studio he happened to end up at. Sometimes, when delivery would be early in the afternoon, they would tell him to plan on staying the next time. All his stories were interesting, and he would tell about the nicest people in the world that he would meet.

I was anxious to go with him, and I had to get "permission" to leave my job for Thursday and Friday. We planned to take the children to Mom and Dad Stanelle. They were happy to have them; and Ken and I were happy to have a few days together. It was like a holiday.

The night before our trip, boxes were heaped in the Cerami-van, and everything had its place. The first studio's supplies were loaded last. The cases of glaze were left in the house until morning, because we didn't want them to freeze in the van overnight. In fact, when we left the following morning at 6:00 a.m., it was so cold that I was sure the air was crackling, and trying to freeze us solid. There was a heater, but I brought quilts to wrap the children in.

We headed north out of Milwaukee, and Ken drove extremely careful to avoid bumps and sudden stops. He didn't want any broken greenware. Finally we were on Highway 41, and he could drive the speed limit without worrying. We dropped off Mick and Peggy, and headed for Appleton which was located in the Fox River Valley.

We unloaded supplies at the Cotter Ceramic Studio. Mrs. Cotter and her daughters operated a very efficient studio where a limited number of students learned the arts. Mrs. Cotter was a member of the Fox Valley Artists Association, and when she was not doing ceramics she was painting. I was especially interested in her oil paintings. I thought she was quite talented, and enjoyed asking about her canvas and the brand of oils she ordered from a catalog.

We got back in the van, and headed for the city of Green Bay. We had to stop at a gas station that had a weight check station, and everything was in order; so we headed for East DePere, which is a suburb of Green Bay.

We stopped at the DorKen Studio, owned and operated by Dorothy and Ken Schroeder. They had a small farm, with a house and small barn. Their old machine-shed served as a garage and ceramic studio. We had a sandwich and a cup of coffee with them, while Ken made out their bill; and then we climbed back into the van.

The next destination was Marinette, Wisconsin; and the owners of St. Onge Studio were waiting for us. Besides the ceramic studio, they had a tourist business and a mail order business. They placed an ad in a large national magazine offering small finished ceramic pieces. This was my favorite stop so far, because over coffee, we discussed the shows, classes, and ceramics in general. Ken was right—people really *were* friendly.

Back in the Cerami-van again, Ken drove extremely careful, as we were well into deer country. Every little curve and hill must be watched closely, and every little movement on the side of the road brought his foot to the brake. The hills were steeper, and curves were sharper. However, the woods were beautiful, with the pines hanging heavy with snow.

We headed north to the Wisconsin-Michigan border town of Iron Mountain, an enthusiastic skiing area. You could see evidence of the sport by looking at the storefronts, and seeing signs advertising everything from winter outerwear to skis to ski-mobiles.

"We would normally stop at Dolly's Ceramic Studio," Ken said, "but tragically, a fire swept through her home and studio; and left her family with the clothes they were wearing. You'll see when we drive by the foundation of her home...."

"I can't help thinking," he added, "that no matter how bad we feel we have it, there is always someone less fortunate."

We kept on driving to Ishpeming, Michigan.

"I don't always deliver to this next studio because of the distance involved, *and* it depends on how much she needs; but I wanted you to meet Mrs. Thebilcock, and see her little studio."

It turned out I was so happy he went there, because she was a delight! Her shop in the basement was small, but she also made jewelry from stones. She was a very *young* eighty-two years of age, and still buzzed around the local shows—*including the one in Milwaukee*, absorbing everything and anything she could see. I wanted to stay longer and visit with her, but Ken nudged me that we had to hit the road.

Our van swung northwest toward Iron River, Michigan to deliver to Betty of Ceramic Cellar Studio. Atmosphere surrounded us as we walked into the basement of their split-level home. The walls were made of huge stones; and a large fireplace, with the fire crackling, dominated one wall.

When we were back on the road, Ken asked me, "What did you think about that place?"

"I thought they had a *beautiful* studio!"

"No, I mean about *them*. I'll never forget that one time last fall, when I stopped. Betty's husband and kids were making their own Christmas tree lights with a soldering iron."

"Did they blow up?"

"I never heard that they did," Ken said smiling. "I'm so glad you could come along. Now you can put a picture to the name when I return from my trips."

On the way back, we stopped at Eagle River, Wisconsin. "In the wintertime, it is composed of only the natives; and in the summertime the streets are so crowded you can barely walk along them," Ken explained. We pulled up to Sadie's Ceramics, operated by Sadie Hugg; and Ken said, "Sadie also runs a tavern and a resort with cabins. Her husband is a guide for fishermen…. This," Ken said while pointing to the ceramics shop, "is a cute studio where her finished pieces are displayed. A buzzer system tells her when a prospective customer walks into the gift shop; and when there's a little spare time to be had, she goes fishing…. You'll see why this is my last stop of the day."

Ken then told me to follow him. He gave me a fishing pole; and we stepped into a boat, which was waiting for us. We fished until dark, and I was getting *famished.*

When we returned to shore, Sadie had a pan of fried fish waiting for us! She also told us which cabin we would be in.

I didn't catch any fish, but Ken caught a walleye and three bass. He exchanged them to Sadie for our cooked ones.

What a wonderful trip. The frosting on the cake was being able to snuggle up to my husband with all the peace and quiet of the world.

After a breakfast fit for a lumberjack, we headed the Cerami-van northwest to a small house, just out of Hazelhurst, Wisconsin. This was where Caroline and her sister, Ruth Dempsey, lived.

Ken said, "They're both retired school teachers, who just can't get teaching out of their systems. Their home and studio are hidden behind a row of evergreen trees; but their talents and hobby cannot be hidden from the people in the area.... Tourists add *volumes* of business in the summer, when they put signs out on the highway."

I was curious to hear how they compared teaching in a school to teaching in their studio. I couldn't seem to get enough of their conversation; but before long, Ken had to nudge me again that we had to leave.

The long journey south went on for only a little way before we made our next stop at Rhinelander, Wisconsin. There, we met the owners of Kay's Ceramic Studio. Ken told me about the couple before we got there, and that George is physically handicapped. He works solely in the studio helping his wife. Ken thought their decision to make a living from their hobby was wonderful to see.

About 100 miles south—our last stop, was Van's Ceramic Shop (near Stevens Point). Their studio is just a little different from most. They both work diligently all winter long, and in the spring. Pete, with his car full, goes out to the various gift shops in the area to sell finished ceramic pieces. This is a real challenge, because the competition is large.

That was the end of the studios for this trip, and Ken would deliver to the studios close to Milwaukee in a few days. We headed back to Seymour, Wisconsin, where we would stay the night, and visit with his parents. They would expect us to go to church with them, and I brought extra clothes for that. After a big lunch with his sisters and their families, we headed home.

What a nice trip and holiday for me.

CHAPTER EIGHT

"You know, hon'," Ken started, "if I had more room to pour greenware, I could sell more."

"What do you have in mind?"

"Well, you remember meeting those couples that make their living with ceramics? *Why couldn't we?*"

"But Ken, we've overextended our basement and garage as it is."

"I know, but we could see if we could find a building to rent that we could afford. Then you could be done with *Mister* Brentmeister."

Of course that made me laugh, and feel a little giddy. I guess it was time to get out the pad of paper and pencil again.

So that night, after the children were in bed, we sat and added and subtracted upside down and crossways, and kept exchanging ideas a mile a minute. A decision was made. Ken would start looking at available places, and I would not quit my job until we knew for sure.

It took about two weeks before he found an ideal place that we could realistically consider, and he arranged for me to see it on Saturday. It was standing vacant on a corner, and had been a drugstore at one time. The street level floor would hold greenware shelves, and the room off to the side would be my office. There was a basement, and Ken thought it would be a good place to do the pouring—which is messy. There would be room upstairs to have a table for teaching. We would keep our Cape Cod house *and* have a business building. *What an exciting time!*

David, our third addition to the family, was now old enough to go to Kindergarten. But Peggy, who was two years older than him—and older than her years, was quite responsible. She was able to wait for him after school, and walk a block to Ruth's house, staying with her until I picked them up two hours later. I just loved Ruth. She was a friend of a ceramics friend, and I trusted her. The children liked her, as well.

Our fourth child, Penny, was just a baby; and I wasn't ready to have her leave me. So we bought an extra crib and playpen, and put it in the office in our new building.

The only one that had to stay home was our dog, Freddy, and he didn't like it at all. He was used to being by Ken's side all day. Later, when we were open for business, Ken would take him down in the studio pouring room. But imagine a black Labrador walking—or even worse, *laying* in clay spilled on the floor. When I saw that, I told Ken, "That will never do." Ken finally found a place behind the store where he could leash him.

We were happy at our new building. Ken was *happy as a clam!* But, he couldn't get enough casting to fill the shelves. Then one night, while we were sitting on the front porch of our house waiting for the students to come, our neighbor Janet came walking over.

"Hi," she said. "What the heck you guys doing? Harold said he saw a lot of commotion over here the other day, with your van going in and out of the driveway every hour. You moving out?"

"Hi Janet," I said. "We decided to go for it. I quit my job, and we rented a store. We've been too busy to tell anyone; and right now we're sitting here, too pooped to participate."

"Hi Sweetie," Ken said, "Want a job?"

"Yeah, what kind…makin' kissy face with you?"

Ken told her what he was doing, and how he was having a hard time keeping up; and she said, "I'll think about it."

Janet was our first employee, and she stayed with us as long as we lived in Wisconsin. She was a hard-worker, she chained-smoked, and she was robust. The whole family loved her. She wasn't fat; she was what we in the Midwest called "big boned"—solid and hearty. I mention this, because any hug one received from her was sure to be a squashing one. When she was home, she wore a dress and a full house apron with ruffled edges, nothing fancy. Her hair was brown, tightly curled, and always set exactly the same way.

Janet was special—and besides that...once in a while she would make a banana cream pie for Ken that you could die for!

****

The casting of the molds was in the basement of the new studio. Carrying buckets of liquid clay, called *slip*, became too difficult. Ken thought about it, and finally came up with *"The Gravity Solution."* He bought a huge barrel, and placed it upstairs to the side of the room and over his pouring tables. Then with a conglomeration of tubes leading down through the floor, and over the pouring table, he fastened a faucet-like fixture on the end. Downstairs, the tubes could be pulled to reach the molds on every corner of the table. With Janet helping him, they turned out multiple pieces of greenware, and filled every shelf.

One time, Janet was carrying up a tray filled with greenware; and Ken, busy with his head down, called out, "If you're going upstairs, take that flowerpot with you."

Janet quipped, "Sure, stick a broom up my *you-know-what*, and I'll sweep the steps on the way up!"

Ken looked up, and saw she had her hands full, and realized what she said. He hooted so loud that customers and I had to find out what was going on! Then Janet got laughing so hard that she almost dropped the tray of greenware.

The whole building shook with laughter.

****

We were busy with the local customers, and the May deadline was approaching. We had a *show* to do! Ken did his designing and finishing of his Drape Mold pieces at our home studio. While I was having a class in one room, our children joined Ken at a table in the other room. They colored or played with their toys.

When David was around three to five years old, we would give him clay to play with; and when it was bedtime, I would have to run my fingers along his gums to remove all the unused clay. I swear he ate the clay genes, and eventually would be a potter by osmosis.

My Tuesday evening class consisted of five students: Laura Jones, Ann Holden, Denise Hoppler, Diane Cummings, and Mary Radue. Laura was prim and very tidy with her work—as well as with her words and smile. Ann was on the quiet side, but really messy with her space and work. Denise was the happy-go-lucky of the group. She could imitate a friend, or character on TV, and had us all laughing. Then she would parade off to the next room to share a joke with Ken. Diane was shy, and could barely have anyone look at her work—even though she had a talent, and was quite good. Mary was the quoter. She constantly told us what she learned about ceramics and kilns and clays.

One night, after leaving the classroom to share a joke with Ken, Denise came back into the classroom, and said, "Hey Shirl, do you and Ken like being your own bosses?"

"Well, Ken would rather be a policeman; but I absolutely *love* it," I answered fervently. "Although I have to tell you, I've never worked harder in my life. Actually, I would never have thought of starting a ceramic studio, or even learning about them, if not for my husband. A few years ago, he found a little ceramic shop on his beat in Milwaukee, and encouraged me to take lessons there…. I guess Ken knows me best!"

I ended that with my hands on my hips, and a little wiggle, and got everyone back to work.

CHAPTER NINE

One day while we were all busy and toiling away, a man came to our shop, and wanted to talk to us. He told us he had a nephew in Sicily named Sebastiano Maglio who wanted to move to the United States. He was an eighth-generation potter. The trouble was he had to have a job promised him before he could get a visa. The uncle was asking if we would give him a job.

We told him we had to think about it, and asked him to come back the next day.

"What do you think, Shirl?" Ken asked. "What would we do with a potter?"

Then, thinking more about it, he added, "You know, Janet and I are just barely keeping up; and if she had help, I could still deliver up north to some of the studios a couple days a week. I wonder what kind of pay he has to have, and if there's a requirement from the government?"

I suggested, "You could have him teach you how to throw on the wheel."

Ken looked at me as though the light just went on. "Wow, you think?"

We asked the uncle a few more questions the next day, and pretty much decided we could make it work.

About two months later, Sebastiano's uncle called us, and told us his nephew had arrived, and wanted to meet us. We were anxious to meet him, too!

It was a beautiful day in April, and we were outside when they pulled up. Ken walked toward Sebastiano, and greeted him with a handshake, saying in Italian, "*Benvenuto! (Welcome!), Siamo felici di incontrarti (We're happy to meet you).*" These were some words Ken had learned while patrolling Milwaukee's East Side, when he was in the police department.

Sebastiano and his uncle got a big kick out of that, and applauded. Ken's Italian was much slower, of course; but the kids and I were truly amazed, and proud of him. Sebastiano broke into a huge smile, and answered, *"Grazie. Sono felice di essere qui! (Thank you. I'm happy to be here!)"*

Sebastiano Maglio was stocky with big muscular arms (from throwing on the wheel), 5 foot nine, with a full head of black curly hair, and a smile from ear to ear. Introductions were made all around; and when it came to Peggy, she tried to say his name but it was just too big a word.

Sebastiano bent down, and in his broken English, said to her "Hey-a Peggy, come-a, give-a me-a beeg-a hug-a…and shust call me *Charlie.*" And we all called him Charlie from that day on. We felt instantly comfortable and happy around him.

It was Friday, and we agreed that Charlie would come on Monday, and Ken would teach him how to cast a mold. He was a charismatic magnet to have around.

Ken could hardly wait for a wheel lesson. He had two months to shop around for a potter's wheel; and it so happened that the manufacturer of our brand of kiln also manufactured wheels. We were able to get a new Skutt Potter's Wheel at our discount.

Ken and Charlie made a plan that the lesson would be each day right after lunch for an hour. Charlie told us that in Italy and Sicily all the pottery was wheel thrown; and if you were a potter, you better keep up, or there was someone in line to get your job.

That wasn't Charlie's case, however. He came to us with lots of natural talent, but he wanted to come to America because he had relatives here. In order to throw at the speed he threw, he was taught to use his arms and elbows by tucking them into his body for support. Most potters that we knew used a brace for a support, which did slow them down.

Charlie taught Ken to wedge the clay in his hands by making a ball, and then throwing it down on the wheel. Then he taught him to use his big hands to center the ball, and pull it up into a cylinder. Charlie shared techniques, such as the kind of handles to add to the piece, and how to finish it properly with a good foot or rim on the bottom. Using Charlie's techniques, Ken would be able to pull up a large pot without a problem. He was a good student, and caught on easily. Pretty soon we were having pottery coming out of our ears.

We started putting original pottery on the shelves, and customers really liked it. That started Ken thinking again. *"Why not make molds of some of the pieces, and have our own originals?"*

When the pot was trimmed and dry, Ken would make a mold of it. To tell the truth, he wasn't bad at making a mold, as long as it was basic and simple. But oh my, what a mess if it was fancier!

After all—he was a potter!

CHAPTER TEN

During the next few years, we exhibited at many different shows. We were so ready to show off our Drape Molds. One day when we were in our little Cape Cod home in Milwaukee, the owners of the Chicago Show called us. Elmer Kane and his wife, Eileen, wanted to take us to dinner, and talk with us. Well, they meant *Ken*, of course.

They came to pick us up in their brand-new, black Cadillac; and parked in front of our house. The neighbors came, and looked at the car; and all the kids ran out to see it. Elmer and Eileen were very charming, and when we climbed in their back seat, we both felt pretty special. We had never been in a Cadillac before.

We knew the restaurants that were the best in Milwaukee, but the one we went to downtown was the *best* of the best. It was a French restaurant, and the décor was beautiful. I had to stop myself from staring at everything.

We sat down and ordered, and Elmer insisted we have anything we want. I had a glass of white wine, and Ken a Brandy Manhattan. Ken ordered a T-bone steak (the bigger the better), a baked potato, and broccoli. I ordered filet mignon, a baked potato, and asparagus. We all had one of their specialty French desserts and coffee. I had a *crème brûlée*, and Ken played it safe by ordering an *éclair*. I don't remember what the Kanes had…. I think Bailey's coffee.

Elmer & Eileen Kane with Fred de Liden, publisher of *Popular Ceramics*

At dinner that night, Elmer asked Ken to put on an event that they could publicize. He heard that Ken had learned to throw on the wheel, and wanted him and his new employee from Italy to put on a demonstration. He loved Ken, and kept calling him his *boy*.

Over the course of the three-day show in Chicago, Sebastiano and Ken created a four-foot pot in our booth. The booth was larger than normal, with space for them to work. They had taken Ken's wheel, lots of red clay, a tarp, and lots of paper towels. One would work on pulling up the clay with his hands, and the other would work the pedal of the electric wheel to make the wheel spin. They took turns blending and pulling it up.

On the last day, they pulled the upper part, and added a coil of clay on the bottom of this new pot with a narrowed neck. More incising and design work, and it was finished. In order to fit in a kiln, the piece was cut below the coil, making it two pieces that would fit together as one pot after it was fired.

Lots of pictures were taken for an article in the Chicago paper, and the Kanes were pleased.

From left to right, the three men are Ken, Fred De Liden (publisher of *Popular Ceramics*), and "Charlie" (Sebastiano Maglio).

****

One time, I overbooked the shows—one in Nebraska and one in Palm Beach, Florida. Ken was to demonstrate at the show in Nebraska, and then teach at two studios after the show. So that meant I had to do the show in Florida. But the problem was we only had one reliable car and our Cerami-van. Ken called his dad, who loaned him a car; and I took off for Florida in our Nash station wagon, pulling a trailer filled with supplies. I had to drive nonstop, because the show would be in three days, and it would take us two days to get there. I took Peggy, who was nine;

and she fed me crackers and snacks while I drove like a crazy woman.

When I got too tired, I pulled over to the side of the road, made sure the doors were locked, and set the little alarm clock for a short nap. The first night, we were in Tennessee, and it was raining and very dark. Luckily, I was able to drive behind a semi. It was my saving grace; and I was very grateful he stayed on the road all the way, or I would have wandered off behind him, and been lost for sure.

We got there with two hours to spare, and Peggy helped me unpack boxes. She saw a friend she knew from other shows, and dashed off while I finished setting up.

The show did well for us, and I kept calling Ken to see how he was doing. He was thrilled that while at his show, two more studios asked him to teach in their studios in other states.

The studios liked to have a teacher, because it gave them notoriety, extra sales, and kept the classes fresh. Usually, the teacher was paid a pre-arranged fee according to the number of students. The more talented and popular the teacher; the higher the fee. Teachers usually had products along that the studio could sell with a fifty percent discount. Some sold stains, some books; Ken sold patterns and Drape Molds.

The show in Palm Beach was doing well, but on Sunday there were warnings of a hurricane heading our way. The hotels started boarding up their windows, and bringing in all the beach chairs and paraphernalia. The show continued, but the customers were getting scarce, and at 1:00 p.m., it was announced that the show was closed.

Boxes were brought up from storage, and I started packing. In the bottom of one box was a big three-inch cockroach. Of course, I had seen a whole kitchen full when we were living in downtown Milwaukee (while Ken was in the hospital); but I still didn't like them, and I wasn't going to take this one home with me. I coaxed a passerby to take the box outside, and dump it; and he did. *Bless him!*

By the time I was finished, the palm trees were bending over, and the tips of the trees touching the ground. Everything got shoved in the trailer, and a tarp pulled on top. Fighting the wind, I picked up a coconut which had fallen to the ground, and hopped inside the Nash. We headed west and northwest until we were sure we were far enough from the storm before it hit. And Hurricane Betsy *did* hit!

Back in Nebraska, Ken heard about the storm, and was frantic for us. I kept stopping at phone booths to call him.

Once Ken knew we were out of danger, he could settle back to his demonstrating and selling.

CHAPTER ELEVEN

One week to go, and we would head to our annual *big* ceramics show in New Jersey. We had been hiring various babysitters to stay at the house; but one day, I read in the paper that a babysitter had suffocated her charges, and that scared me. Not that we had any problems before, but I wasn't going to take any chances. I told my friend Arline my tale of woe; and the next day, she called saying, "Hi, I spoke with my mother, and now that she's widowed, she wouldn't mind earning a little. She can watch the children while you're gone to the shows."

We met with her, and agreed to pay her $100.00 per week. It was stretching our budget; but the kids were safe, and she took good care of them.

At this time, we had a newer car—a 1965 Pontiac station wagon, and Mick would attend the show with us. Thirteen-year-old Mick came home from school one day, and in answer to our, "Hi Mick," he flatly told us, "My name is *Michael*."

"O.K.!"

Michael was a great help with loading and unloading the product and the big supply of Drape Molds that were made for the show. Ken had a scheduled time to demonstrate; and always after the demonstration, our booth had customers standing three and four deep to purchase the molds. Ken, with Michael's help, talked and charmed yet another group of people.

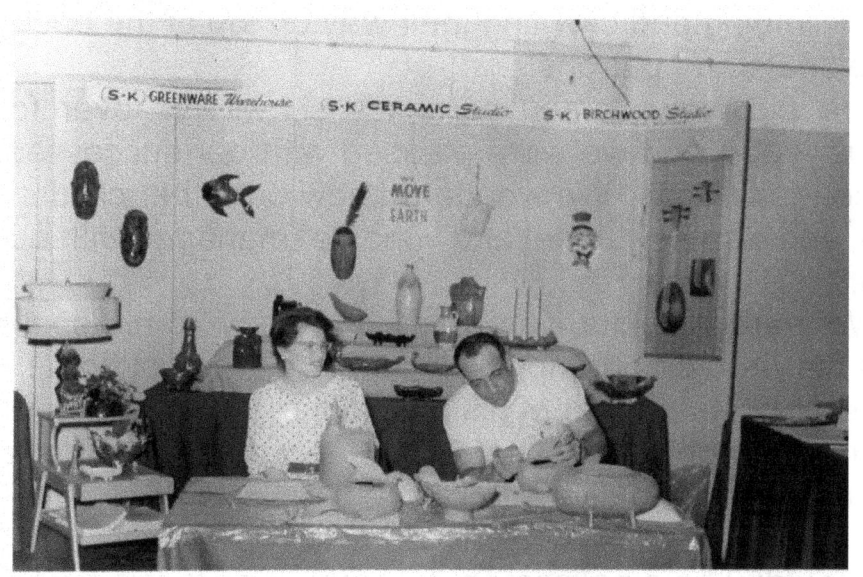
Shirley and Ken in their show booth

This time Ken had enlisted mold-maker Fred's help, and planned on going to his workshop before we headed home. Ken told him on the phone about Sebastiano, and throwing on the wheel, and wanting to make a mold of the pottery pieces. Now he wanted to know how to make the masters to sell to studio owners. Soon, we would have molds to sell of Ken's original wheel-thrown pottery.

This was Michael's first trip to the East Coast, and we decided to take a one-day trip to New York. As each child reached thirteen-years-old, he or she was allowed to accompany us. We let them choose what they wanted to see or do on their first special day in New York City. Being a teenager, Michael's choice was to see *Hair*, the new musical playing on Broadway. The only tickets available were *standing room only*. There was a designated place for us to stand; and the "standing checkers," would come along, and make sure we were in the right spot. The most memorable for me was the way the actors got up to the stage. They approached right next to us, climbing and crawling their way on top of the backs of the seats and patrons!

The big New Jersey ceramics show was over for another year, and we were pleased with our successes. We headed home. We wondered how our other children were, and also how Janet and "Charlie" managed with our shop.

We were thankful Ken didn't have any of his spells while we were on our trip. He waited until we got home, I guess, to have another of his blackouts. We should have avoided ever going anywhere, but Ken wouldn't hear of it. He wasn't going to give into it.

If he couldn't be a policeman, he was going to live his life as fully as he could.

CHAPTER TWELVE

Back to his shop, Ken used his newfound knowledge to make molds of the pottery and masters (molds of molds).

The Lord's Supper, made with Ken's original mold.

This new phase in his life never quit. Ideas of new things just kept jumping out of his head. It was a time of change. For one thing, Ken, a hunter, criticized the favorite sportsman magazine of the time. "Look at this. They make it out as though the hunter *always* gets his game. I wish they had stories more true to life." Then he looked at me, and said, "I think we should write our own magazine—a truthful one."

A friend of his worked at a printing plant, and knew the *ins and outs* of printing, and the proper lingo we would need to know. So, together they took out a loan to get it started.

Our bookkeeper advised against a monthly, suggesting we do a *bi*-monthly. We should have listened, because we didn't know that all the big advertisers want you to be published a year before they advertise. *But*, we put out a very nice magazine called *Wisconsin Horizons*.

After six issues, we saw the reality of the whole thing, and Ken offered it to the local newspaper. They planned to buy it, and use it as their supplement; but then the racial unrest of the country hit the streets.

It was 1967, and the newspaper felt it wasn't the time to expand.

****

In addition to this blow, our landlord gave us notice. He said he finally was able to sell our business building; and he was sorry, but that was life, and we had to be out in a month. A friend let us use a space in his building, and the mold-making was moved there until we found bigger quarters.

Since we lost the possibility of making big sales, *and* we had to have the funds for a new place, we had to let Charlie go. I guess you could call this "The Domino Effect"—one thing goes down, hits another, and a downward trend continues.

Ken sent a wonderful letter to all the major ceramic studios (who, incidentally, were secretly *lusting* over having Sebastiano). We felt bad, but we finally found him another place to work. He didn't last there too long, however. Haeger Potteries of Dundee, Illinois plucked him up *for their very own,* and he stayed there eighteen years. He became their traveling artist, to promote their products; and would demonstrate wheel throwing at the biggest and finest stores around.

We looked and looked, and finally Ken found a three-acre place in Germantown, a suburb north of Milwaukee. It had a farmhouse, machine shed, and a barn. A transformation started—a new home, a different studio, new schools, a different church.

However, unbeknownst to us, it was a small change compared to what was to come later in our future....

CHAPTER THIRTEEN

Ken made arrangements with a well-known sculptor named Corky to purchase her cute and popular figures for a mold. We made four in a mold, and called them "Corkies." When cast with slip (liquid clay), they were used as an ornament, or they could be applied to other pieces of greenware or pottery.

It was a huge success! We offered over fifty mold choices. It was a craze, and the other mold companies hadn't caught on yet. During this time, we learned that the greatest success could come from shipping—*and boy did we ship!* Back then, we shipped with newspaper pushed inside of the shipping box in an accordion manner (forward and backward v's). This accordion configuration separated the molds, and kept them from shifting. Ken's dad would come over, open stacks of newspapers for Janet, and she would pack the boxes with such care that we never once had a complaint of a broken mold. We were all very proud of this.

The first year, we sold out of Corkies, and decided the next year to go for broke. We rented a semi-truck; and Michael took lessons, and passed the test for his commercial driver's license, so that he could drive to the various ceramic and pottery shows.

At one of our shows that year, we bought three booths, and had seven people manning them. We made up colored brochures of the finished pieces; and on a small piece of paper, we placed the number and pictures of each one.

People were standing six deep, and when they got up to the table to be waited on, they had their choices all made up. We totaled them, they paid, and we sent them out to the truck, where Michael found the molds for them.

This was a far cry from our *first* show—when all we sold was paper patterns. In stark contrast, we all met in our motel room the first night; and, sitting around the bed, the money bags were opened, and spilled out. After counting mold numbers and money, we all yelled with joy, "$20,000.00 in CASH!"

We were ecstatic! It was in 1969.

Our Corky Brochure

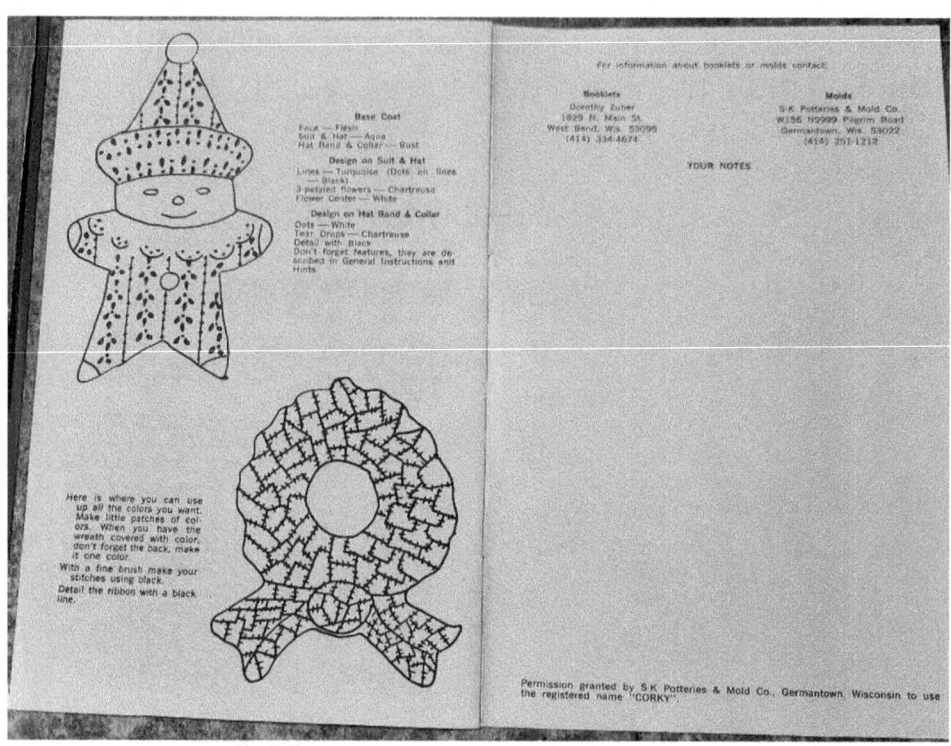

Inside Back Cover of Corky Brochure

CHAPTER FOURTEEN

The farmhouse in Germantown was a little roomier than our Cape Cod. It had a kitchen, which we promptly decorated with a built-in double oven and an island with a stove top. Wallpaper covered the old ceiling; and when you looked up, it was to the underside of mushrooms. A dining room and living room were downstairs; and bedrooms were all upstairs except Michael's, who opted to make the once used chicken coop as his personal bedroom.

The machine shed was used for the mold-making. It had an upstairs, which held my office, and also the supply of masters. I no longer had classes, and only needed a pouring table to make a sample. The downstairs was the actual mold-making business—now run by *thirty-two* employees!

Germantown Farm

Janet became our shipper and taskmaster. She kept the guys at work—including Ken. If the tomfoolery lasted too long, she'd crack the whip, and make them all get back to work. She could be a little gruff, but she was a softy inside. Her family only ate certain foods; so she would make *short order* meals for them based on their preference—one dish for her son, one for her husband, and another for herself. We teased her about that.

Janet Gust

We were amazed at how much she spoiled them.

****

The barn was not used yet. One day, Ken coaxed me to leave for a short trip. "You have a secretary now; you should be able to leave."

"Where are we going?"

"To Illinois."

Ken had been doing some checking, and found out that the Germantown farm area did not have a local clay-maker. The schools and potters were getting clay sent in from Minnesota and Missouri.

Different clays have different purposes. There is a *ball* clay for elasticity, another clay to withstand higher temperatures, etc. The various types of clay come in powder-form, and you mix them just like making a cake. There was a big mixing-machine called a *pug machine* for sale in Illinois, and we were going down there to look at it.

It was beautiful day, and I have to admit, it was nice to get away. It was especially nice to hog my husband for myself for three hours each way.

Well, we bought the machine; and Ken took charge of the task of getting it to Wisconsin. It was a huge monster, and filled up a good deal of the barn. Ken had arranged to have on hand bags of dry product to produce several types of throwing clay. We now had *ball* clay, *fire* clay, and "*kaolin*" (usually used for making porcelain). These put together in the right proportions would create the perfect *working* clay.

The top of the machine had an opening to pour in the mixture of the batter, so to speak. Ken found a used forklift and a tank, which would be placed in the upstairs loft of the barn. The forklift lifted the bags of powdered clay up there, employees opened the prescribed number of each kind of clay, and dumped them in. Water was pumped up there, the clay was mixed, and then transferred to the top of the pug machine. Out from the pug machine came the clay in the shape of a rectangle. It was chopped off at a certain point to make a twenty-five pound *lug,* or chunk of clay. A different machine put the lug into a plastic bag, and it was ready for sale.

Another part of our business—a clay company.

****

The mini-farm brought more additions—beagles, another Labrador, a horse for Peg, a pond in front of the barn, and *parties.* One year, while the big show was in Milwaukee, and the vendors were from all parts of the country, we decided to have a party, and invite anyone who could find us. Ken got his creative juices going again, and built a wood floor on the driveway that ran between the machine shed and barn. Then he made a huge barbeque station to be used for roasting the wonderful large ears of Wisconsin corn. A band was arranged, and a mystery hunt planned. Guests would be in teams, and had to find the hidden clues. The hidden clues were rhyming-riddles which Ken wrote, and each clue led to another one. They were hidden throughout our three acres. The team that finished first would each be given an excellent piece of pottery we had made.

The night finally arrived, and everyone was given a torch or flashlight. The corn was roasting, and the band was setting up to play…. And then it started to rain. Not rain, but *pour.* Everyone gathered in the small room next to the pug mill—including the band. Shortly after the downpour subsided, the band began to play; and the guests talked and laughed. We finished partying in a very crowded fashion; but afterwards, the party was dubbed as "the best party anyone ever attended."

Life was good.

CHAPTER FIFTEEN

Clubs, associations, and schools are always looking for a good speaker—especially one that could *also* entertain. It didn't take long, and Ken was on a speaker path. He could *throw* on the wheel, tell stories, and just about anything you needed, he could do it, and do it willingly.

One time, we were at a fancy dinner that a show was putting on, and we were seated at one of many round tables all dressed up. We were having a cocktail with other ceramic friends when a man approached Ken, and whispered in his ear. Ken nodded his head, and disappeared. I had no idea where he went until the curtain opened, and out stepped my husband.

"Good evening, ladies and gentlemen. I am here to inform you that the MC has been detained, and I am your MC for tonight."

Applause and cheering.

Ken then proceeded to tell a joke, and introduce our entertainment. Neither one of us knew I would be dining most of the evening without him....

But getting back to local engagements, he got a call from a high school art teacher that had taken lessons from us to get extra credit. She wanted Ken to do something to help boost attendance in her art classes. He told her he would get back to her within the week. Later that week, Ken presented several ideas to her. The teacher agreed. He then asked her if she had a student with a good sense of humor that could be his *"model,"* and that she not tell a soul what was going to happen. The teacher found a likely student, and Ken would perform the following week.

The week went quickly, and he began to load the Cerami-van. In went the potter's wheel, two big garbage cans, a folding table, a stool, two lugs of clay, two rolls of paper towels, lace curtains, and finally one finished and one *un*finished porcelain doll.

He arrived at the school 30 minutes early to give himself time to unload and set up all his equipment in the gym. He was just finished setting up, when the students started filing in from the art classes. *But,* there were more students than he had planned, because other classes wanted to join in, as well. The gym bleachers were *full!*

"Hello, ladies and gentlemen. My name is Ken Stanelle, and I am a potter. I am here to tell you, and show you, that the arts—including *pottery and ceramics,* can be fun and creative…. It's not just a slough-off class."

Everyone cheered.

Then he went to his potter's wheel. "The reason everyone says he will *throw* a pot is because after the potter has kneaded the clay, he *throws* it on the wheel, forcing the air out between the wheel-head and the clay, so it can stick there. If he didn't do that, and started turning the wheel, it would fly off, and hit someone in their T-shirt."

Ken demonstrated.

"Next step is to *pull a cylinder.* Every potter does this necessary step, because it is the beginning of a great pot. It is the forming of a great foundation—like kindergarten or elementary school."

Ken continued to throw a pot the size of a large cantaloupe, and the audience cheered.

"Now the difference from a potter working with clay, and a ceramist in a studio is this: A potter works with raw clay on a potter's wheel; while a ceramist works with molds and slip in a ceramic studio. Molds are cast, and a figure emerges…like this porcelain doll." Ken held up the finished porcelain doll to show the high schoolers what he was talking about.

"This doll was cast in porcelain slip, which is a special clay powder with water added. It is mixed like making a cake, and then poured into a mold.... Now, when a doll like this is available, the ceramist wants to dress it, and must put the material into clay slip, and form it around the doll. If he didn't put it into the slip first, the material would burn up in the kiln."

Ken looked up and across the bleachers, and said, "I can see some of you are confused, and maybe I can demonstrate with a volunteer to help you understand.... Young lady in the first row with the pink T-shirt, would you come up, and be my model?" *A dozen hands had shot up, but Ken knew his model would have on a certain pink T-shirt.*

She came up, and he had her sit on the stool.

"What's your name?"

"Mary Ann."

"Thanks for coming out here to help me, Mary Ann.... Now let me continue. To get material to stay.... Wait a minute.... Let me first show you how to make a flower out of clay."

Ken proceeded to take little pieces of clay, and form a flower about four inches in diameter. He could make a clay flower just as fast as he could make a frosting flower when he was a baker. It was large enough, so he could lift his hand, and show it to the students. "We'll just put this over here. You never know when you may need a flower...."

Ken then took a large piece of lace. He dunked it in the barrel of slip. While dunking the lace, he said, "Back to dressing the doll...." He pulled the lace up to reveal that now the slip coated it. He squeezed and stripped off some of the excess slip, and said, "This is what I meant when I said the material must have clay slip on it, or it would be burned off. The material will still burn away, but the clay coating either side of it will remain. Let me show you."

He proceeded to wrap the large piece of wet, slip-coated lace around Mary Ann's waist and legs while everyone in the room gasped. Now they were *really* paying attention.

"Let's see, I still have a little lace left."

He dipped it in the slip, squeezed it out, and put it over Mary Ann's shoulders.

"See what I mean?" he asked. "If she were a ceramic doll, and I put her in a kiln, the material would burn up, and the clay would remain."

All this while Mary Ann just sat there patiently, without moving. Ken moved all around her, and finally said, "I think she looks a little plain."

Laughter everywhere echoed in the gymnasium!

Then he went to the wheel, and took off the pot he had thrown earlier. He added a large piece of clay to the top of the pot to make a wide rim. He returned the pot to the wheel, and said, "Remember what I said earlier: First you *throw;* then you *pull* the cylinder."

His pot grew and grew, wider and wider on the top; and now the kids were catching on. They were screaming!

He took the wide-rimmed pot off the wheel, walked over to Mary Ann, and placed it on her head! Then he shaped the pot over Mary Ann, saying, "I need to make it look *just right....* Wait a minute.... Remember what I made earlier?"

The students were yelling, "The flower! The flower!"

Ken picked up the flower, and put it on Mary Ann's new *"hat,"* saying, "Another ceramic doll in the making!"

Ken then pointed to Mary Ann, so that she could receive applause.

Shortly after, Mary Ann slipped off the stool; and ran for the showers, where she had clean clothes waiting.

The next semester, the art classes were full.

CHAPTER SIXTEEN

One day, in the middle of all life's chaos, Ed and Roberta Gensch stopped by, and excitedly told us about their free trip to Colorado.

It was November 1969, and McCulloch Chainsaw Company was developing their second city, *Pueblo West*, in Colorado (their first was Lake Havasu in Arizona). To inspire folks to purchase a lot for investment purposes, they provided a round trip *Electra-Jet* flight, fine meals with warm Western hospitality, and a tour of Pueblo West. The weekend included a beautiful room, dinner, and breakfast.

"You should go," they coaxed us. "You two are stressed out from working around the clock."

"Yeahh, well, when do you think we would have time to go…like for a vacation?"

Well, we finally agreed to go, and contacted McCulloch; but we didn't know when we could do it. Each week, we had to put off the salesman; and then one time he brought McCulloch's first newspaper which shouted, "*Fly* to COLORADO…without cost to you!"

We decided it was time—maybe just to stop him from begging us to go.

We went, and had a nice weekend; but we said to the salesman who showed us the land, "It's all very nice, but we can't invest for a home, because we need to find a place for our ceramic business."

That was very true. Ken had just gone into the town council, and they refused to let us operate on our road in Germantown any longer. They denied the renewal of our license.

They had other plans for the land adjacent to Pilgrim Road.

****

Two weeks later, we heard from the Colorado people again. This time, they asked us to consider looking at moving our business there. Repeated plane trips flew our family, our employees, and even our lawyer and accountant.

One year later (with five loaded train cars), and we were living in Colorado. What an extreme change in life—from lush, deciduous trees and conifers to prairie land, *with little or no trees,* lots of wind, tumbleweeds, and sunshine. But, it was a chance to watch a new community grow.

We felt God had a hand in this decision-making. A church had formed, and met in various small places; but it ended up meeting in our very own lunchroom for six years until land was purchased. Every Saturday, congregation members came, put up chairs, moved a table out of my office, and a stand from the shipping department. They put down a rug made from carpet samples for the children to sit on.

Newcomers or visitors were told, "Don't wear black to church because you might get clay or plaster dust on you, and it will show."

Most people move to Colorado because they had been there on vacation, or liked the skiing. It was a brand-new state for us. In fact, when we announced in *Ceramic Magazine* that we were moving, our publisher called, and said, "You kids know that is the home for many Mafia members?"

We had never heard of Pueblo before, so *"Big deal."*

We had perfect credit records, and were able to acquire a loan for a lot and a building in Pueblo West. We planned to build a 20,000 square-foot building instead of the 40 "*thou*" that our credit allowed.

Colorado was our new home.

COMPLETING arrangements recently to bring SK Potteries & Mold Company, Inc. of Milwaukee, Wisconsin to Pueblo West were Mr. and Mrs. Kenneth G. Stanelle, right, and Eugene Lemmon, Pueblo West project manager. A $200,000 manufacturing facility is going up east of Aspen Skiwear as new home of the pottery and mold firm.

S-K Potteries & Mold Company, Architectural Drawing

GROUNDBREAKING ceremony for the $200,000 S-K Potteries and Mold Company, Inc. facility had Kenneth Stanelle, company owner, removing the first shovel of dirt at the plant site. Holding a drawing of the facility are Charles Martz, Mrs. Stanelle and Ron Wadleigh. Martz is the city's industrial development representative and Wadleigh is superintendent of Pueblo West's physical plant department.

S-K Potteries at a Distance

Our twenty thousand square-foot building was built, and ready for us to move into before we arrived; and our 35 new employees had been hired. None of our Wisconsin employees could make the move, but my secretary and Janet came to help us train and set up various departments.

S-K Potteries Close-Up

Our building was set up for producing new blocks and cases, a shipping department, kiln room, offices, and manufacturing. The front would eventually have a gift shop and an antique shop.

Ken and Shirley living in a mobile home while their house was being built.

Ken had always wanted a trophy room; so with savings from his pension, we had a house built on a mesa. We rented a mobile home until it was finished. Meanwhile a moose was hanging on the wall in the lunchroom/church until the house was built.

CHAPTER SEVENTEEN

After a few years in the S-K plant, our yearly totals were added. We devised a goal of a quarter million dollars to appear in the books. Before we knew it, we only needed six more dollars.

In no time, we achieved our goal—$250,000! It was the *only* time; but the family celebrated. My youngest daughter remembers that all the kids received a small portion. She said she remembers feeling so rich—even though it was probably just for new school clothes. David remembers getting his first mini-bike.

****

S-K Potteries was the first in the industry to introduce Southwest pottery. I remember many times that Ken would be throwing on the wheel with a Native American grandmother standing in front of him, and directing him as he completed the piece, while her grandson interpreted for her. We made molds for them to cast in exchange for the original Native American designs—especially the Native American wedding vase.

Native American Wedding Vase

The traditional method of a wedding vase by an authentic Native American was built with many coils of clay. It had a bulbous bottom, and then it worked up to two sections. The two separate tubes were joined together with one big coil of clay. An avid collector could reach inside the pot, and feel the coils of clay to know it was authentic.

In the wedding ceremony, the man would drink out of one spout, and the bride out of the other. The looped handle, joining both spouts, represented the unity achieved with the marriage.

Now the Native American art dealers were pretty *savvy:* It was fine to sell to a collector, but most tourists didn't really care. I don't know how they heard about Ken, but someone told them. If they could get a mold, and cast it; they could finish it more rapidly, and sell more.

One of our original wedding vases is still being sold to this day, but they are now collected for the designs applied to them. Each had their own style. The Acoma tribe was very distinctive. The designs dictated the price.

I believe Ken's work helped the Native Americans achieve monetary value; and the Native Americans helped Ken achieve success, also.

****

Beyond the excitement of the dollar success and collaborating with Native Americans, we had tours of school children. This was right up Ken's alley! Our son, Michael, was our master mold-maker; and our daughter, Peggy, was our tour guide.

Peggy remembers her dad telling the touring kids, "When I start throwing on the wheel, start counting *ONE, TWO, THREE.*"

The children would go *"One, two, three,"* and bingo—the pot changed shape. They would go, *"One, two, three"* time after time; and the shape of the pot kept changing on each count of three. The children's shrieking and laughing rang throughout the plant.

One day, for fun, Ken picked up a cholla branch from the prairie; and that day the kids on tour cut out simple shapes from the clay to be fired and hung from the branch. They were to return the following week, and put them together to form a wind chime. Ken's samples were always hung in the gift shop, and to his utmost amazement, they sold *every time!*

The wind chimes became a new adventure. He searched for and used pieces of cactus to pieces of driftwood. So when the spring river-flows would send pieces of wood down from the mountains through the Arkansas River, we were there at the dam's reservoir to pick them up.

Always trying to improve, Ken created a formula for a source of clay that would produce a musical tone instead of *"Thunk, thunk......."* With a newly modeled bird or squirrel, and molds made from the originals, a new design was created. We called them *Colorado Wind Songs*, and started selling them at art shows and Renaissance Festivals.

Our son, David, decided to quit his job, and make these chimes for a living; and then Peggy and her husband; and finally Michael, who created designs featuring Alaskan wildlife. It is a good thing the chimes were a constant seller, because the ceramic studios became a "thing of the past." The ceramic industry was a baby in the fifties, and came into its own during the sixties and seventies. Then plaster items and resin took over, and in the eighties the industry as we knew it, disappeared. *Quit!*

Luckily, the Native American pottery and windchimes managed to survive. Ken's pottery and the Colorado Wind Songs are still being produced today.

Colorado Wind Song

Visit www.colorado-windsongs.com.

S-K Potteries & Mold Co., Inc.

Located 8 Miles West of Pueblo on U.S. 50

KEN'S KOLLECTABLES AND ANTIQUES

A new addition recently opened is Ken's Kollectables and Antique Shop. Two large rooms of nostalgia captures the era of yesteryear and a bit of Colorado history. "My mother had one of those," and "My father threw one of those away," are familiar comments heard daily. Among the mysteries of the past you may find that little treasure you have been looking for.

Another refreshing feature is that all items are plainly marked, and at reasonable prices. After all, this isn't downtown Chicago. As you enter the Antique Shop, you are requested to say "hello" to Ralph so he isn't offended. Until someone buys it, the Victor talking machine will belt out the Wabash Blues for you while you browse.

There is a lot of mañana here in the West, and no better place to do it than in Ken's Kollectables and Antique Shop.

HOURS:
Monday - Friday: 8:00 - 4:30
Saturday: 10:00 - 4:00
Sunday: Closed

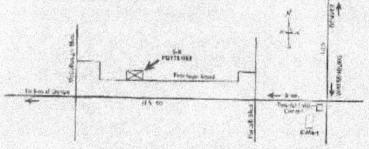

With all the things you can see under one roof at S-K Potteries, you wouldn't think we would have any time for ourselves. Well, you're right!

TELEPHONE 547-3322
275 E. Enterprise Dr.
Pueblo West, CO 81007

S-K Potteries Brochure (outside)

DESIGNERS AND MANUFACTURERS OF ORIGINAL ITEMS

S-K Potteries and Mold Co., Inc. is uniquely different from a regular pottery plant. It is here that molds for the ceramic trade are designed and created for other companies.

The making of molds is an interesting and complicated procedure. However, the steps from sculpture to finished product is simply explained during your tour. Molds are the backbone of the ceramic and pottery business and good designs are always in demand. Questions are cheerfully answered, not only by your guide but from our employees as well. This is not just a tour but an education in mold making.

COLORADO WIND SONGS

S-K Potteries is the home of the Colorado Wind Songs which are hand made and tuned so that no two are ever alike. Driftwood from the prairie floor, lakes and streams are hand selected, to which stoneware chimes are added to create a symphony of song by nature's winds.

It's never a question of wanting one, but always a difficult question of which one you want. These creations of sound will give you a lasting memory of your visit West for years to come.

By the way, the really smart shoppers take several along for their friends back home.

FOUNTAINS

Even though our original fountains are for the more discriminating buyer and a little difficult to take with you, be sure to see them all. Sculptured by Robert Festerling, a noted Colorado artist, they are cast in cement for lifetime pleasure.

Some of these castings in the molds weigh over a ton and are quite an engineering job to produce. If you just cannot live without one, we do ship them and in many cases deliver them. Our trucks are constantly on the road from one coast to the other and often times they are delivered to your door.

Having one of our fountains in your yard or patio settles the age old race of keeping up with the Jones's once and for all.

POTTER'S WHEEL

Wheel thrown pottery dates into biblical times, and is one of the oldest forms of art. Little has changed except the equipment used, and Ken Stanelle has a unique way of using it.

A constant stream of information comes during his demonstrations which delights young and old alike. His humor and quips, along with personal conversation, cannot hide his superb mastery of the wheel. Pieces that meet his approval are all signed by him personally and are tastefully displayed in the Earth 'n Art Gift Shoppe located in the front of the plant. The selection may be small as mass production is almost unheard of at S-K Potteries.

This behind-the-scenes tour will delight everyone in the family.

S-K Potteries Brochure (inside)

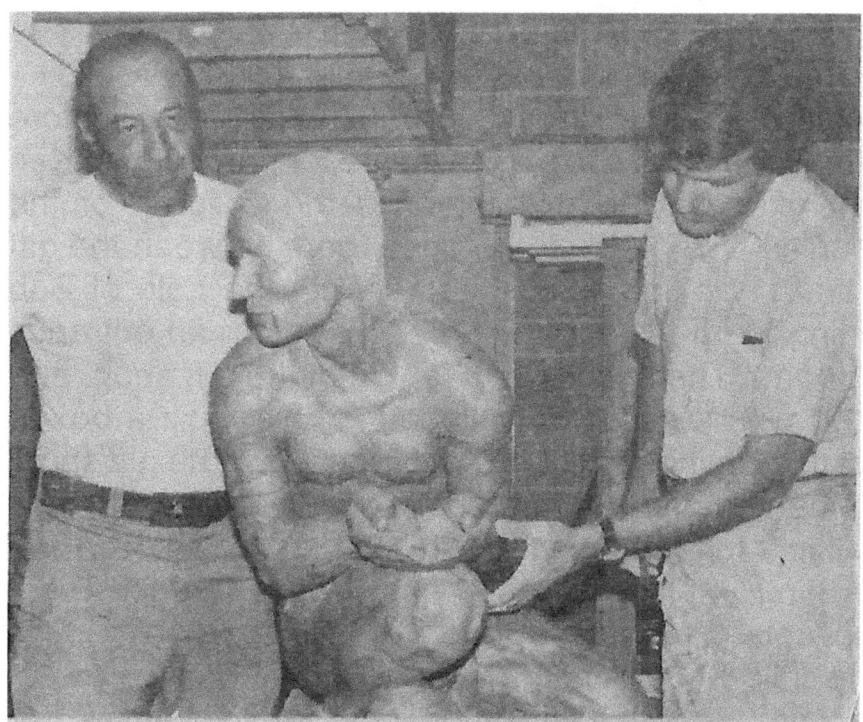

Bob Festerling, right, is the artist of this beautiful Indian fountain statue. The cement statue is made only at S-K Pottery and Mold in Pueblo West. Helping engineer the statue is Ken Stanelle, owner of the pottery shop.

Our resident artist, Bob Festerling, had his studio in our plant.

CHAPTER EIGHTEEN

Most of our orders were shipped out before Christmas, and that gave a downtime for production. Ken thought of a way to give back to the children of the community. We had a conference room between the gift shop and my office. So, together with the help of Bob Festerling, our resident artist, Ken designed an entrance to the room. The door was taken off of the gift shop, and replaced with a sheet of wallboard. They built a box in front of it, creating a child-sized opening into the gift shop. They did the same with the door going from the gift shop into the conference room. Bob painted scenes on the whole thing, making tunnels; and the conference room was now our "Secret Gift Shop."

Any child who could crawl in the tunnel was welcome. Inside the Secret Gift Shop, our employees—*now "Santa's helpers,"* helped the children shop for items that did not exceed $3.00. We made as many items as we could think of that we could sell for a low price; and we also went to Merchandise Mart, and bought multiple gifts in that price range.

Once in that room, and gifts were picked out, the chilldren crawled through the entry into my office, where *"Elves"* wrapped the packages. The children finally came out with gifts for *Mom and Dad,* fully wrapped for Christmas.

Also, either while they were waiting to enter or when they came out, they could dip a candle, and take it home for themselves. The candle-maker sent us a metal tray that heated the various colors of wax, along with an order of small white candles.

The finishing touch was *"Santa Claus."* Ken's dad, Grover, came to Colorado, and looked the part of Santa with his large frame and belly. He donned the Santa suit, and children climbed on his lap to have their picture taken.

Grover Stanelle (Ken's Dad) as Santa

It was a magical time.

CHAPTER NINETEEN

On our travels to many shows, Ken loved to stop at any—*or all*, resale shops. Finally, I suggested that, as he was accumulating so much *"stuff,"* perhaps we should partition a section of the building into an antique shop, and so we did. We papered the walls with old newspapers, and it looked the part. We called it *"Ken's Collectibles and Antiques."*

One day, as I was back in our gift shop arranging jewelry, a tall, distinguished-looking man came in, and stopped to see what I was doing. He looked familiar to me—like somebody possibly famous, but I couldn't place him. His wife had scooted into our new antique shop.

I looked up, and stammered, "Are you somebody important?"

"Yesss," he slowly answered with a big grin on his face; and he turned away from me, and followed his wife into the antique shop.

Meanwhile, one of our employees saw him, recognized him, and ran and got Ken. It was Ricardo Montalbán (of the television show *Fantasy Island*) with his wife, Georgia!

Ken quickly came, full of clay and plaster. He followed them into the antique shop, and introduced himself.

Ricardo was in Colorado shooting a film in the mountains, and they were taking in some of the local sights. Soon they returned to the gift shop, paid for their purchases, and Ken said, "Well, we'll see you tomorrow night then. I'll put on the steaks."

He invited them for dinner!

I think they must have been bored between movie takes, so they came. We had a wonderful time together.

Later in the week, Ricardo's wife Georgia, invited our daughters to have lunch with her.

****

There were less than 1,000 residents in Pueblo West, and our place was a hub for many events. We had fundraisers for the church. Spaghetti dinners were a favorite, and pretty much everybody in the community attended. Camp stoves were brought in, and pots of water heated on them. I don't know where Ken drained the pots of spaghetti; but it was great, and so was the sauce. Mostly, it was a place for people to gather.

Ken used to eat lunch with the employees, and the men enjoyed having Ken taste another *"hot"* (spicy) Pueblo chili dish. Our employee, Felix Gallego, always brought leftovers in a rolled-up tortilla—leftover potatoes, eggs, veggies, or whatever. Sometimes he would warm it up in the microwave or not. It didn't matter to him.

Ken immediately pounced on that idea, and another fundraiser was in the making. We made signs, and we called them *"Breakfast Tortillas a la Gallego,"* named after Felix. I believe we were the first to call them a breakfast tortilla, and it was another big success.

It was a busy, fun time; and Ken made the most of it. He and three other men who loved to sing got together and formed a "barbershop quartet." Eventually, they added a female voice, and called themselves *Misfires and Friends.* It wasn't long, and their singing engagements led to several a month.

There were too many things to elaborate on, but Ken joined the Gunslingers, the Sportsman League, the Pueblo West Economic Development Association, the Men's Golf Association, and the VFW. He was director of our local bank board, and yet he always found time to hunt and fish.

Ken was an intriguing figure to write about, and there were many newspaper and magazine articles in the next 10 years telling about him, and what he was doing.

Life was good…except when he had a blackout.

****

One day, Peggy and I were in the bedroom to check on Ken. He was recovering from an operation, and we were asking him something. He started fading, and I started screaming, *"Ken! Don't leave me!"*

Peggy immediately picked up the phone, and called the ambulance.

Another time—*the worst,* was the day he returned from an examination by our doctor. After entering our building, he walked into my office, and I was shocked at how pale he looked. He sat down on the couch, and I asked, "What happened?" And the next thing I knew, he was on the floor.

I opened the door, and screamed, *"Michael, come quick!"*

Michael yelled to a few employees, and they all came running. My secretary quickly called 9-1-1, and an ambulance was on the way.

The ambulance arrived in minutes, and they put Ken on a gurney, and into the ambulance. I climbed in, and sat next to him. Michael drove behind us in my car.

The closest hospital was eight miles, and the ambulance siren was blaring. All of a sudden, Ken's moaning increased; and every few seconds, he would call out something which I did not understand. Just like that, his hand went to his throat where he had been cut, and he was trying to hold it together. He was reliving the knife/gun fight.

The ambulance attendant and I both leaped forward, and pulled on his arm. It took all the strength we could both muster to pull his arm away from his throat. *Would he have choked himself?* That time, his blackout was so severe that he had to stay in the hospital overnight.

Michael drove me back to the plant, and all the employees wanted to know about Ken.

CHAPTER TWENTY

Things would always calm down, and we tried to go back to normal. He started to give lectures and talks with his potter's wheel, as he did before in Wisconsin. One Sunday, when we were without a pastor, he decided to give a talk about his life in abbreviation. He called it, *"Why Me, Lord?"* His talk paralleled God's control over our lives with the potter and the clay. Ken would say, "Many times, things happen, and we have to start over again. Sometimes it's harder the second or third time...."

News travels fast. Once organizations and churches hear of a speaker—*especially one with a unique message,* they seek him or her out. One of the engagements brought a reporter, and soon I was busy setting up engagements for him. If it was in a church, his basics on wheel throwing referred to Sunday School. If it was a business organization, then the basics were compared to Kindergarten. When the national campaign was on *"Just say no to drugs,"* then he was asked to speak on that to schools and prisons.

He never followed a written copy, as he was an extemporaneous speaker. Each talk was a little different. Whatever the audience, it did not matter, he always ended his talk with these four words:

PICK UP THE CLAY

The following is one of Ken's inspirational talks that I was able to pull off a recorded tape:

KEN'S TALK

Over the years, when I gave this talk, I would call it *"Why Me?"* One time or another, most everyone has asked this question, *"Why me? Why me, Lord?"*

I grew up thinking my family was very rich. When I was fourteen years old, my father gave me $4.00 to take the North Shore train from Milwaukee to Chicago, so I could visit my cousins. When I got there, I realized I was poor. I thought everyone lived as we did.

Growing up, I knocked around at various jobs until I finally got what I liked, and that was being a policeman on the Milwaukee Police Department. The Chief was picked from the ranks of the department, and I had every reason to believe I could be Chief someday. Of course, there were one thousand fifty men that thought the same way.

I started out as a beat cop, and then driving a squad. Then I was put on the undercover duty to learn and understand how it was to be out of uniform. My thirty-day stint as an undercover cop turned into three and a half years. I enjoyed being someone I was not. One of my favorite stints was when I was an Italian, and answered to *"Stanelleee."*

Life was good. Every month, Shirley would take my paycheck of $228.00, and divide it into envelopes with $4.00 for gas, $10.00 for utilities, and $4.00 for a vacation, etc. Life was going on just wonderful.

And then one Thanksgiving night, we drove through *"The Hole."* The Hole was not a place that ordinary citizens visited—it was railroad tracks, taverns, and just a rough area. As we approached the Old Mill Tavern, two men began to drag a third man between them, a woman followed close behind.

We stopped to question them, and in a matter of what seemed 30 seconds, I had to kill a man, shot another in the leg, and busted a woman's face. *In a space of 30 seconds, everything I worked for was gone....*

I made my way to a call box to call in the incident, and ask for help.

When a call comes in that another officer needs help, every other arrest is put on hold, and they all race to help.

Men came in on all angles....

Well, I made it. But, due to my injuries, I was no longer allowed to work as a policeman.... But I was alive. It was a very difficult time in my life, and I asked, *"Why me, God? Why me?"*

In the Bible, the clay cannot question the potter any more than we can question our maker. In Isaiah 64:8, it states, *Lord, you are our Father; we are the clay. You, the potter, and all of us are your handiwork.*

You hear about *"throwing"* pots, and that is exactly what it means. After the potter kneads the clay to get the air out, he "throws" the clay onto the wheel causing a suction. That is the first step.

The next thing the potter must do, is center the clay. Not, just a little centered—*right in the middle.* The potter then pulls the basic cylinder. This is like going to kindergarten—or bible study. The clay goes up, and he fashions with pulling the clay out here or there; and now he is smart. "I am an accountant," "I am a teacher," or "I am a firefighter."

Now comes the *real* education. The potter has made a beautiful pot, and life is good. *HERE, though, THE POT CRASHES DOWN.* Something happens we didn't count on. A tragedy. What is a tragedy? It can come in different forms. It could be a knock on your door at midnight telling you about an accident your son or daughter was in; or it could be the little girl that was wearing her new dress to church, and fell, and got it all dirty. To *her*, *that* is a tragedy.

We all have those days, but what are we going to do about it? The hospital in town has a *"Penthouse"* on the fifth floor—full of folks suffering from depression....

What does the potter do? Every day, his pot may not be right, or he pulled the clay when he shouldn't.... But he just picks up the clay, and starts over. The clay is a little more soupy now, but it still has to be wedged, and the air worked out. When it feels about right, then he is ready to start over again. He throws the clay on the wheel, prepares to make a cylinder, and begins to reshape the pot.... *Just like we can reshape our lives.*

As long as you have your mind, you have everything.

I had to change, even though I didn't want to. I was laid up in hospitals for seventeen months off and on. It was not my lucky day. When they told me I couldn't go back to work, and I had to turn in my badge and gun...it really hurt.

Another example are our soldiers who go off to war; and nothing serious happens until one day, their barracks is raided, and it is one-to-one battle for their lives. One soldier kills a man. When that soldier comes home, he will need support, because nothing can take away the feeling of killing a man.

I was given the highest medal of the year. The only one higher would have been posthumous, and given to my wife—and I didn't want *that* one.

God answers prayers, but it is not always what we want. Maybe *He* wanted me to do something else.

Accept the Lord's Prayer. *Thy* will be done.

I like to tell the story of the man who fell off the cliff, and was hanging onto a little branch sticking out. He called, *"Help!"*

God answered, "Let go."

The man thought a second, and called *"Anybody up there?"*

He did not receive the answer he wanted....

Then there's the story of the pastor who was ready to retire, and he wanted a place for his horse:

> The pastor took the horse to a ranch; and asked the ranch owner, *Charlie*, if he could leave the horse in his pastures.
>
> Charlie said, "Sure pastor...no problem."
>
> The pastor then asked, "Could you ride him once in a while, so he doesn't get too lonesome?"
>
> "You bet," Charlie answered. "We'll get along just fine."
>
> The pastor explained, "If you ride him, he *goes* with the words 'Praise the Lord,' and he *stops* with the word 'Amen.'"
>
> So the pastor left.
>
> When he was gone, Charlie got on the horse, and said, "Well, we are a going to get acquainted, so *Giddy-up.*"
>
> The horse just stood there.
>
> This time Charlie really yelled, *"Giddy-up!"*
>
> The horse still stood there, so Charlie proceeded to whip him until the horse took off with him, and they were galloping down the pasture.
>
> Charlie thought, *"That's more like it,"* until he realized that there was a 16-foot arroyo, dried up waterway, with a deep drop to the bottom, at the end of the pasture.
>
> Charlie yelled, *"Whoa! Whoa!"* and the horse kept going.

Finally, he remembered what the old pastor told him, and yelled, "Amen! Amen!" and the horse stopped inches from the rim of the drop-off.

Charlie, took off his hat, wiped his brow, and said, *"Praise the Lord!"*

Ken paused to allow his audience to realize what had happened *and laugh*. Then he continued his talk:

Being a Christian is not easy. You're supposed to love your enemies.... I have to tell one, last story:

Mary went to Heaven, and wanted to get in; but was refused. She was outraged, and started complaining, "Wait a minute. I went to church every Sunday; and I certainly gave my share of money to the church. I demand that you check your books again."

So the angel checked his books, and said, "You are right. You went to church every Sunday for one hour, and you will be able to come in to Heaven one hour a week...."

Speakers come and go. I always think they have something to say, and try to catch little gems, and file them away. One missionary gave me something to file away. I hear him say, "We can't all be missionaries or pastors, but we *can* all be witnesses for God...."

How you grade me is unimportant. When you are down there, and feel you are in the gutter, and don't think you have a friend; just remember these four words:

PICK UP THE CLAY

Thank you everyone, and God Bless.

****

Ken was a gifted artist and speaker. Several times he was asked to speak at the *"penthouse"* of the local hospital. It was a floor of mentally disturbed or depressed patients, who were being treated. One of the times, he was told that "Mary" would not attend; and in fact, would not get off her dolly in the hallway. After his presentation, he asked to use a spare dolly. He climbed on, rolled on his stomach, and headed down the hallway after her.

"Hi, Mary," he quietly spoke. "I'm really disappointed you didn't come to hear me...."

I never knew what he told people, but I would hear about the results....

Like the nurse in the penthouse saying that Mary started coming back to the group after Ken spoke with her.

What did he say?

Like the time a young friend fell from a high scaffold, broke his legs, and was terribly depressed. His parents were financially comfortable, and could arrange for most any kind of help, but nothing worked. We went to visit him and his parents, and Ken asked to see him alone. He went in his room, and shut the door.

The young man recovered, and went on to run his parents' very successful business. They always said it was because Ken spoke with him.

What did he say to him?

I will always remember when we were sitting by the roadside at a small craft show, when a young boy about sixteen ambled over to Ken, and said, "Mr. Stanelle, I just want you to know that I'm better now."

The young man had been at a youth prison camp, which was one of the places Ken spoke at occasionally.

What had Ken said to him?

CHAPTER TWENTY-ONE

My friend, Anne, *who worked for us,* and my daughter Penny told what happened one day when Ken joined them in their part of the studio. Ken clasped his head in his hands, and leaned over the slab roller.

Penny knew the signs, and yelled, "Anne! Get a cold, wet towel, *quick!*"

Anne quickly returned with a towel, they put it on Ken's neck, and just held his hands.

Over the many years, Ken knew when a spell was coming on, and sometimes he could fight it off. A few minutes later, he would come out of it. The neurosurgeon had told us that the spells, caused by the head damage, would eventually weaken his heart to the point where he may not survive one.

****

It was a few days before Christmas of 1994, and our store, Earth'n Art, *in downtown Pueblo West,* was really busy. I was downstairs putting out samples of a new product, and the gals from upstairs would let me know when the phone was for me. Ken called about four times that day. He was making last minute Wind Songs to bring to the store. The last time he called, he wanted to know when I would be home. All these times of running up the flight of stairs, I never fussed about it. I told him, "around seven," and he said, "Good, I'll go swimming, and then visit Chuck, from Church; because he's not feeling well."

That evening when I got home, we had a fat belly-hug; and I made supper of rice pilaf, salmon, and green beans. We ate, watching a television program called *"9-1-1."*

I told Ken that I had to work in the studio to load the kiln one more time. I suggested he join me, and watch TV there to keep me company.

"Okay," he replied. "But first, how about some ice cream?"

I didn't usually, because it wasn't my big thing; but it was his, and I said, "Okay."

Then, before he got up, he turned, smiled, and said to me, "I...*Love* You."

My head had a spiral go up from it, and I thought, *"What? Where did that come from?"*

He walked right behind me, and around the counter, to dish up the ice cream; and I turned back towards the TV.

I heard a big thump, and turned around calling, "Did you drop the ice cream?"

He didn't answer, and I ran around the counter.

There Ken lay on his back...dead.

CHAPTER TWENTY-TWO

My employees took care of the store until I could do so a week later. When I returned to the store, customers—*after giving condolences,* asked what happened.

I told the story over and over and over again.

It was nine months before I finally sat down, and wailed, and grieved.

Ken always filled the room when he entered. I was always just happy to be along. How was I going to go solo?

I did what Ken would have wanted me to do....

I **Picked Up The Clay**.

About the Author

Author, Shirley Elaine Stanelle, was born February 8, 1928 in Green Bay, Wisconsin. Kenneth Grover Stanelle was born January 12, 1928 (at home during a snowstorm) in Woodville, Wisconsin. The two were united in marriage on November 27, 1948 in Seymour, Wisconsin.

Shirley says that her life with Ken was always interesting and challenging. When he died unexpectedly, she knew she would be going "solo," but Ken's words, "PICK UP THE CLAY" encouraged her to move forward. She took courses towards becoming a master gardener; she enrolled in a week-long watercolor class in Mexico; and she continued to work at EARTH'N ART.

Out & About Magazine featured Shirley, and described her gift shop EARTH'N ART as "A unique and wonderful store on B Street in the Heart of Pueblo's Historic District."

One day, on her way home from EARTH'N ART, while walking along the Arkansas River with her little Shih Tzu companion, Miss Muffitt, she saw boulders along the sidewalk, memorializing loved ones. She thought, *"How nice it would be if my family would do this when I join Ken."*

"Then," Shirley declares, "my Holy Spirit...*loudly and clearly*...said, '**Build a memorial garden!**'"

"It was loud, just like hearing aids when the battery is almost gone, and they shout, *'Battery!'"*

She went to the church, and explained this to her pastor who merely responded, "See if you can find a place."

She did, and in the year 2000, she presented a rough plan to committees (she had never done anything like that before), and formed a group of workers she now calls "Gardenin' Angels." The first section was dedicated in the fall of 2001; and today the Garden has tripled in size to almost two acres with about 67 memorials.

Shirley has started her memoir, *RICH GIRL, POOR GIRL, RICH GIRL*. The first part of the story details her life as an only child, living happily with her mother and father. She felt *rich*. The second part of her life began at age eleven when her mother passed away. She felt *poor*. Finally, the third part of her life began when she met Ken. During this part of her life, *because of Ken*, she has felt the *richest* of all—in mind, body, spirit...and then some!

Beyond the memoir, and *Pick Up The Clay*, her life is full with grandchildren's graduations, births of great-grandchildren, and of course, Paradise Memorial Garden (http://www.paradisememorialgarden.org/), at which Shirley invites you to join her for her annual "Afternoon Tea."

Ken and Shirley's Children

David (left) lives in Pueblo West, Colorado, and has one child, Julian. Like Ken, he is a potter, and produces various-sized Colorado Wind Songs, or "Windsongs," and a specialty line of mugs. He sells them at Renaissance Festivals and art fairs; and his website is: http://www.colorado-windsongs.com

Penn (top) lives in the mountains, an hour from Pueblo West, near Westcliffe on a 40-acre ranch with her husband, Cordin, and three sons, Maximilian, Beauregard, and Wulfgar. Penny is building a seed company, and her website is: pennandcordsgarden.org.

Michael (right) lives in Palmer, Alaska (since 1981). Like Ken, he is an outdoorsman, enjoying hunting, fishing, and archery. He produces "*Ultra* Colorado Wind Songs," and sells them at art fairs.

Peggy (bottom) lives in Pueblo West, Colorado. She is married to Larry Kramer, and has two children, Kenny and Cydney. Peggy worked for the Pueblo DOC (Department of Corrections) headquarters for 15 years, and has been the chef for the annual Tea fundraiser, to provide funds for the Paradise Memorial Garden.

Shirley welcomes your e-mail. You may contact her at shirley.stanelle@gmail.com

Also Recommended by Fame's Eternal Books, LLC:

Fame's Eternal Camping-Grounds: *The Civil War Battles Fort Donelson, Shiloh, & Vicksburg*

Second Lieutenant George Dodd Carrington: *Civil War Diary*

and **the Companion to** *Pick Up The Clay*....

Autobiography of a Successful AUTARCHIST:
Inventor / Adventurer with Milwaukee Roots
The Life of Larry Douglas Gensch

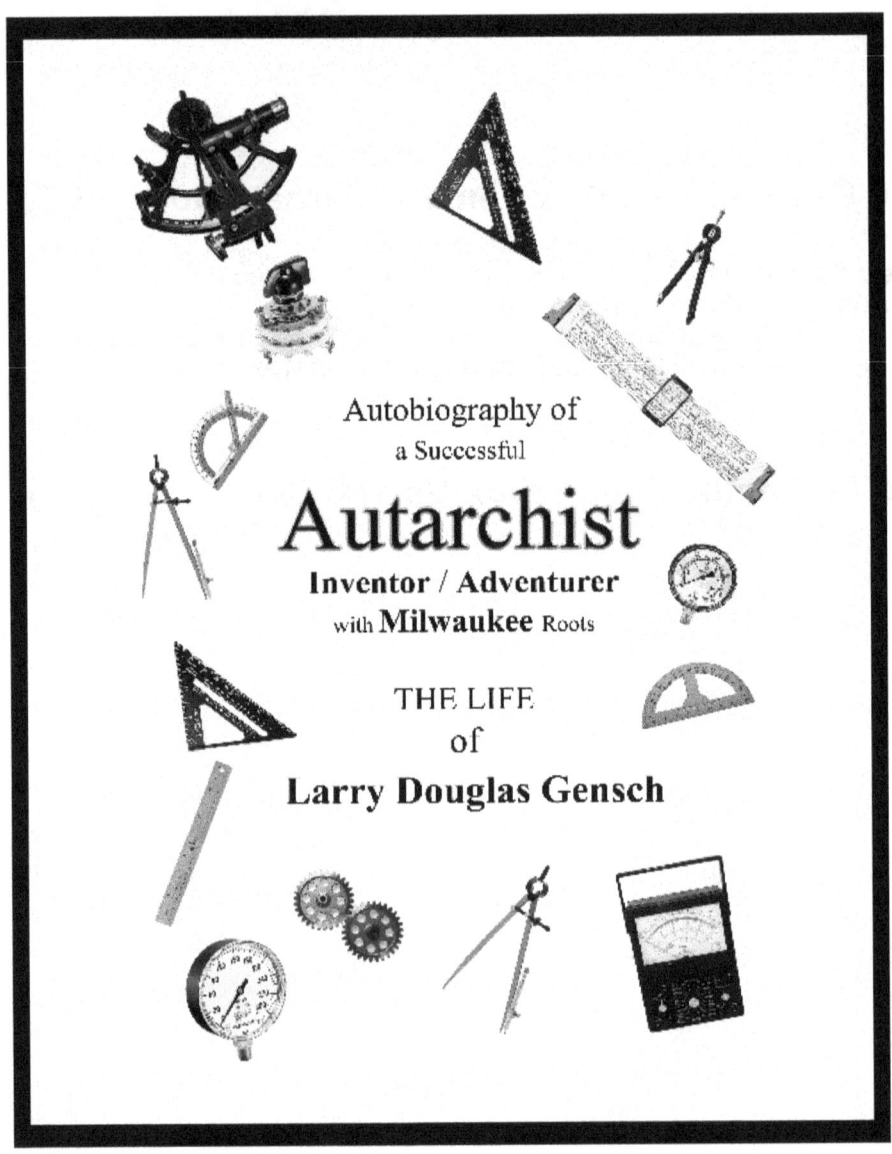